100 Prayers where YOU are

Prayers for life's situations and seasons

Denis Duncan

Pen Press

© Denis Duncan 2013

All rights reserved

No part of this publication may be reproduced, stored in a retrieval system, or transmitted in any form or by any means, without the prior permission in writing of the publisher, nor be otherwise circulated in any form of binding or cover other than that in which it is published and without a similar condition including this condition being imposed on the subsequent purchaser.

First published in Great Britain

All paper used in the printing of this book has been made from wood grown in managed, sustainable forests.

ISBN13: 978-1-78003-498-0

Printed and bound in the UK
Pen Press is an imprint of
Indepenpress Publishing Limited
25 Eastern Place
Brighton
BN2 1GJ

A catalogue record of this book is available from the British Library

Cover design by Jacqueline Abromeit

DEDICATION

This book of prayers is dedicated to my much-loved daughter,

CAROL,

who, very sadly, died on February 7, 2012.

Carol often led the intercessory prayers in her parish church.

Always popular and very talented, she was, professionally, a dedicated teacher, serving as Head of Sixth Form in a large comprehensive school. Pivotal in our family life she will always be remembered with gratitude and love.

Foreword

The concept of "100 Prayers where YOU are" is rooted in the BBC newscasters' regularly referring, when the local or regional news is to follow, to "The News where you are". The prayers which make up this collection are my efforts to put myself in a hundred different situations in which you, the reader, might be. Some are happy, some sad, some everyday, some seasonal and some within the spiritual life. They are not my personal prayers, though they do draw on my personal experience. They are genuine, objective attempts to express what might be an appropriate prayer for you, if you find yourself in one of those situations. So there will be prayers that are wholly relevant to "where YOU are", and there are those which relate to situations in which you have not been: but somebody else is, or has been, there. Some prayers for particular seasons are included too.

My hope then is that some prayer will be the prayer that is needed "where YOU are" at some time in your life.

Denis Duncan

Contents

Section 1: 1-16   1
WHEN ALL IS WELL

(1)	When all is well	3
(2)	At home	4
(3)	In the garden	5
(4)	On moving to a new home	6
(5)	On a country walk	7
(6)	Down by the riverside	8
(7)	On recovering from illness	9
(8)	After a birth in the family	10
(9)	On a birthday	11
(10)	When there is a wedding in the family	12
(11)	Before going to a concert	13
(12)	After an evening at the cinema	14
(13)	In the days of my youth	15
(14)	In mid-life	16
(15)	On returning from holiday	17
(16)	On renewing acquaintance	18

Section 2: 17-39

IN DARK AND DISMAL DAYS

(17)	At the end of a bad day	21
(18)	When we receive disappointments	22
(19)	Facing the mystery of suffering	23
(20)	"When sadness fills my mind…"	24
(21)	When someone has let me down	25
(22)	When you suffer loss	26
(23)	When depressed	27
(24)	When over-worked	28
(25)	When passing through "the dark night"	29
(26)	In a time of doubt	30
(27)	In the depths of despair	31
(28)	"When in the night I sleepless lie…"	32
(29)	When in severe pain	33
(30)	When seriously ill	34
(31)	When harshly criticised	35
(32)	When a relationship ends	36
(33)	When broken-hearted	37
(34)	On suffering rejection	38
(35)	If you live alone	39
(36)	When you are in debt	40
(37)	On hearing of a natural disaster	41
(38)	In a time of war	42
(39)	When someone takes their life	43

Section 3: 40-64

SUNDRY OCCASIONS

(40)	On getting up	47
(41)	Before a medical appointment	48
(42)	When in hospital	49
(43)	Before an operation	50
(44)	On sitting examinations	51
(45)	Before an important test	52
(46)	On accepting office	53
(47)	Before a public address	54
(48)	In advancing years	55
(49)	On deciding to seek counselling	56
(50)	When called to jury service	57
(51)	When gardening	58
(52)	When facing big decisions	59
(53)	After an evening at the theatre	60
(54)	On reading the daily newspaper	61
(55)	On writing a letter of condolence	62
(56)	When family members emigrate	63
(57)	On retiring	64
(58)	Approaching a General Election	65
(59)	After a visit to the library	66
(60)	When frustrated by technology	67
(61)	Before writing a book	68
(62)	Before going to the dentist	69
(63)	On a visit to the Holy Land	70
(64)	By the Sea of Galilee	71

Section 4: 65-85

TIMES AND SEASONS

- (65) At the changing of the clock as Spring approaches — 75
- (66) When Spring has come — 76
- (67) "Summer suns are glowing…" — 77
- (68) In the Autumn — 78
- (69) At the changing of the clocks as Winter approaches — 79
- (70) "In the bleak mid-winter…" — 80
- (71) In the season of Advent — 81
- (72) As the season of Lent begins — 82
- (73) On Mothering Sunday — 83
- (74) On Maundy Thursday — 84
- (75) On Good Friday — 85
- (76) On Holy Saturday — 86
- (77) On Easter Day — 87
- (78) On Ascension Day — 88
- (79) At Pentecost — 89
- (80) At the season of All Saints — 90
- (81) On Remembrance Day — 91
- (82) On Christmas Eve — 92
- (83) On Christmas Day — 93
- (84) On New Year's Eve — 94
- (85) On New Year's Day — 95

Section 5: 86-100
IN THE SPIRITUAL LIFE

(86)	When spiritually drained	99
(87)	When disillusioned with life	100
(88)	When facing temptation	101
(89)	With a guilty conscience	102
(90)	On a retreat	103
(91)	When prayer is not answered	104
(92)	When prayer is answered	105
(93)	Before reading the Bible	106
(94)	Before going to church	107
(95)	Before Holy Communion	108
(96)	After worship	109
(97)	On renewing commitment	110
(98)	When in group meditation	111
(99)	In the eventide	112
(100)	A Benediction	113

Section 1: 1-16

WHEN ALL IS WELL

(1) When all is well

This, O God, is a day that you have made, so I will rejoice and be glad in it. For me, for now, all is going well, truly well. My health and that of my family is good. The work in which I am engaged is creative and stimulating. My leisure time is varied and enjoyable. Blessed as I am, O God, what more can I ask? For such blessings, Lord, I give you thanks.

When you created the world, you saw that it was good. Alas, Lord, that world is now "a good thing spoiled".* And so, within your world, good and evil are in constant conflict and, as a result, suffering abounds.

I gave you thanks, Lord, for that which is good. I have my share today, but I am, at the same time, all too conscious of the prevalence of evil. So, while I have the right to what is good, I also have the responsibility to pray for victims of evil. How violent is our world today Lord! How cruel men and women can be!

That all is so well with me must never make me smug, Lord. It must rather teach me true humility. To be so blessed while others hurt so much, must always move me to sympathy and service.

I thank you, O God, that for me all is so truly well. To those for whom there is only pain and suffering, let my heart be moved to compassion.

In Jesus' name, Amen.

---

*A phrase coined by the late John Baillie, author of A Diary of Private Prayer and Invitation to Pilgrimage.

(2) At home

What a blessing, O God, is the gift of a good home! How truly grateful we must be if home is a place where love dwells, if we have parents who are an inspiration to us, if we have a disciplined freedom to develop our gifts and skills, if we are encouraged to live lives of quality and usefulness. And if these favours are ours, grant us the grace to care for those who are denied these graces.

When Jesus was brought into this world, O God, he came to devoted parents, and a humble but holy home. Cared for by Joseph, a man of God, sensitive to your will, and Mary, loving and strong, our Lord had every opportunity to grow in grace and simple holiness. Schooled in a trade, he worked with his hands, but all the time he exercised his mind, pondering the great truths of life, becoming more and more spiritually aware.

I give you thanks for the home from which Jesus came, for that father so intuitive where Jesus' welfare was involved, that mother, deeply spiritual and wholly devoted to a son, unusually conceived. I thank you for the understanding Mary brought to the bringing up of Jesus, always conscious of his unusual nature, always ready to "ponder in her heart" what she could not wholly understand.

I give you thanks, too, O God, for that home in Nazareth that, in your providence, so shaped the life of Jesus.

I ask this prayer in Jesus' name, Amen.

(3) In the garden

How good, O God, it is to be in my garden. It is for me "a thing of beauty and a joy forever". For the gift of a garden, I give you thanks, O God.

As I saunter round my garden, Lord, I recognise that gardens had a part to play in the Bible story. That the Bible begins with a garden, somehow suggests that gardens have a place in the divine economy. As I recall the story of Adam and Eve, and their fall from favour, Lord, I recognise in their arrogance and false pride how easy it is for me to be self-dependent and feel no need for divine help. How foolish they were, Lord.

I move in reflection to another garden, where the great drama of the New Testament is being played out, the garden of Gethsemane. As in my mind the scene unfolds, I see Jesus kneeling in prayer, his dozing disciples nearby, pouring sweat "like drops of blood" as he wrestles with the purpose of his mission, crying out: "Not my will, O Father, but yours, be done". Rising up from prayer, Jesus goes towards the death he knows he must not avoid, a death for all mankind, a death for me, Lord. There surely cannot be a garden more sacred, more holy.

But there is, Lord. It is the garden of the resurrection, the place of triumph, the site of victory! Like Mary Magdalene, mystified but convinced, I gaze, in imagination, at the empty tomb, turn round and say, in wonder: "Master". What garden on earth can know such privilege, Lord, for it is in this garden we meet the risen Lord.

As I ponder these things, I give thanks for that garden, and for my garden too. For there I can be alone with you, my God.

In Jesus' name, Amen.

(4) On moving into a new home

"Bless this house, O Lord, I pray." I recall these words from a familiar song, and make them my own, O God, as we move today to a new home. How hard it is to leave the house that has been our home for many years. It has such memories, Lord, its happy events, its sadnesses, its familiarity, its warmth and comfort. But circumstances change as do our needs, and I stand, Lord, on the threshold of somewhere which, in due time, will feel like home again.

How difficult change can be. Familiarity can breed contempt, Lord, but it also brings reassurance and a sense of security. The house we are leaving has been home to our children for the whole of their lives. They went to the local school, they attended the parish church and Sunday School. Their friends lived nearby. The shops they knew were on our doorstep. But now they are grown-ups, Lord, and must make their own homes, have their own children, form their own circle of friends and we must, as they say, Lord, "down-size". The time for decision has come. As we move into our new home, Lord, grant us your blessing, I pray.

Give me patience, O God, as I try to get used to unfamiliar surroundings, different noises, new neighbours. May I not idealise and sentimentalise the past and its experiences, but grasp the opportunities a new location offers for creative engagement with new people. Inspire in me the enjoyment of exploration and the delight of discovery, adding to my knowledge, broadening my mind, extending my experience. And, in later life, may I look back and see the step we have taken, not as a reluctant necessity but as a positive, forward move that brought us added blessings.

"My times are in your hand", O God. In all life's changes, may I see your providence at work, Lord, and aware of that providence, may my heart be at peace.

Through Jesus Christ, my Lord, Amen.

(5) On a country walk

How true it is, O God! The heavens do declare your glory! The earth is indeed your handiwork! How gloriously fortunate we all are to be surrounded by the beauty of the earth, to be living under the glory of the skies. To be on a country walk, alone with nature is indeed a blessing, Lord.

Whether it be in the glory of the spring, under the glowing summer suns, or in the splendour of a lovely autumn, I always want to lift up not only my heart but my voice to give thanks for all creation. And not only do I wallow in the magnificence of the trees, shrubs and flowers as they burst into life in spring and reach their splendid peak in the summer. I so relish their garments of gold as they fade into the autumn twilight of their lives. How moving is nature's cycle, Lord! When winter comes, all nature will fall asleep in order to emerge with new life when spring comes round again.

I hear a movement in the bushes, Lord. A rabbit perhaps? A bird preparing to fly up into the blue sky above? A friendly cat? A frightened mole? How varied is your creation, Lord! And entertaining too! I sometimes think you made the living world with a smile on your face, Lord, so interesting and intriguing are the birds of the air and the beasts of the field! How strange it must have been in Noah's ark, Lord! A microcosm of your created world! A created world you wanted to preserve... and did!

As I wander through this lovely day, so surrounded by beauty and life, I am moved to humble thanksgiving for the wonder of it all, Lord. You so rightly saw that the world you had created was good and, although the innate sin which blights humanity has made that world (I say again), "a good thing spoiled", so much of that goodness remains, a witness to the redeeming love vouchsafed to us in Jesus. To be here is for my good, Lord, and for that blessing, I give you my thanks.

In Jesus' name, Amen.

(6) Down by the riverside

For this day, O God, I give you thanks and praise. Here I am, down by the riverside, for a day of rest and relaxation.

O Lord, you made "all things bright and beautiful" and all around me is the splendour of your created world. The banks of the river are grassy green, the "river running by" is clear and peaceful, the sky above is blue and, for this short time at least, all feels well with the world.

But, of course, it is not, Lord. How awful is the contrast, Lord, between the little world where I am "down by the riverside" and the great world beyond it. I give thanks for this little world around me today, Lord, as I pray for the ravaged world outside.

How well Jesus knew the quiet world of retreat. His Bible spoke of green pastures and still waters. His stories were about sheep, shepherds and sheepfolds, a little man up a sycamore tree, a fig tree that was failing to produce fruit. But it was in a quiet place like the garden of Gethsemane, his chosen place of prayer, that that cruel world from beyond it broke in. Led by Judas, they came with swords and staves, the so-called authorities of his time, sacred and secular, to arrest him. It was there serenity and brutality met. That other world was not far away, but fearsomely present.

As I think on these things here and now, "down by the riverside", and marvel at Jesus' courage and commitment in the face of sheer evil, I pray that, for this brief time, I may be granted the privilege of enjoying your creation, deriving from it the strength and peace that I need to live in that other world to which I have to return.

In Jesus' name, Amen.

(7) On recovering from illness

That I am well again, O God, is a ground for gratitude and praise. I thank you for medical knowledge and experience, for drugs that may ease pain and improve moods and for the outstanding skills of modern surgery. Thank you too for the patience and cheerfulness of the doctors, nurses and orderlies who looked after me and made me grateful for the National Health Service. For the many nationalities that compose the modern hospital, I give you thanks, too, O God.

I pray that if there are lessons to be learnt from my illness, I may give attention to them; if there are ways of living that I must leave behind, give me the strength of will that I need to abandon them. Enable me to review my attitudes and aspirations in the light of my recovery and make the garment of humility my spiritual attire. Help me to see in my return to health an opportunity for growth. Let me never forget the healing that comes from a calm and serene outlook, and may a great unselfishness on my part lead me to look more kindly on others' needs.

I now understand much more the nature of true wholeness. I see it clearly as the health, not only of my body, but of my mind and soul. Graciously grant me a fit body, an alert mind and a soul at peace, so that I may go about the business of living with a new zest. O God, use the memory of my illness to encourage me to be truly well. Then shall my sickness become, in your unfailing love, an instrument for my good.

Through Jesus Christ, my Lord.

(8) After a birth in the family

A new life has come into our family today, O God. How grateful I am that the birth has been safely achieved, that baby and mother are "doing well", and that there is joy throughout my family over the addition of a family member. Thanks be to you, O God!

What a miracle the birth of a child is, Lord! How carefully nature takes a mother through the months of preparation, the pain of labour, the excitement of delivery! What hopes cluster round the new life! What pleasure there is for those who are responsible for a new creation! It is indeed a time for humility and reverence, for thanksgiving, for renewed commitment. It is a life-enhancing experience.

With the gift of new life comes responsibility for the whole family, Lord. For the parents life can never be quite the same again, as the duties of parenthood begin to make their presence felt. There may be some things to be given up to make room for things that now become priorities, but there will be much compensation in the new experiences parental responsibility brings. For grandparents there will be all the joy of a new life, without the obligations they knew so well as parents. For the whole family there will be the duty of prayer for the new life, given by God in trust to those who will be called "mother" and "father".

This, O God, is a memorable day for us as a family, a day of thanksgiving and a day for personal re-dedication, remembering as we should that "a little child shall lead them".

Through Jesus Christ, my Lord, Amen.

(9) On a birthday

For the gift of life, I give you, O God, my thanks and praise as I mark another birthday. How gratefully I look back and reflect on your providential care, your unfailing love. You have led me through green pastures and by still waters. You have, over and over again, "restored my soul". And you have been with me in the dark valleys, sustaining me, lifting me up, giving me back my peace when, under stress and strain, it has been taken from me. On this day when many will say to me "Many happy returns", I say to you, Lord: "For the goodness and mercy that have followed me through life, I bless and magnify your name".

May I now welcome another year, generously given to me, as an opportunity for greater service and more effective ministry in whatever way my personal ministry is expressed. May I miss no chance to be a blessing. May I graciously receive the blessings that come to me.

As "one more step along the world, I go"* may I do it with energy, enthusiasm and a will to achieve, not seeking material possessions but rather looking for an "abiding city", a place in which I can be at peace with myself and with others, the added blessing being your gift of peace within. And if a further birthday shall come, help me, like your servant Abraham, of old, to once again go out not knowing where I am going, but full of faith in your purpose for me.

Through Jesus Christ, my Lord, Amen.

*A line from the late Sydney Carter's poem.

(10) When there is a wedding in the family

O happy day! It is indeed a happy day within our family, O God, for today brings about a wedding that we have long anticipated and to which we have greatly looked forward.

As parents, we have always hoped, O God, that our children would find the right partners. Today we feel that just that has happened and the first one of our children to marry is very fortunate indeed, Lord. I could not wish for a better partner for our child, Lord. I hope that his new "in-laws" feel the same about their child's choice.

In days when attitudes are greatly changed, I still value the institution of marriage far above other so-called partnerships. A lifetime commitment, solemnly undertaken in your presence, Lord, provides the right kind of foundations for life. Marriage is "for better, for worse, for richer, for poorer, in sickness and in health" and vows taken "before you and this congregation" seal that essential commitment. I am grateful, Lord, that those who are being bound together today with cords of love share that conviction and want to take such vows. I know, O God, that doing so will stand them in good stead for the years to come. It is my belief, Lord, that marriage, solemnly undertaken, is essential for the future health and well-being of society.

That those who are within my family choose to take the better way is ground for great thanksgiving, Lord. The way they have chosen to have this marriage take place gives me a sense of pride, Lord. O, happy day, indeed!

In Jesus' name, Amen.

(11) Before going to a concert

I pause to give you thanks this morning, O God, for the gift of music. I look forward, with eager anticipation, to the concert I am planning to attend this evening. Music has always had charms, Lord. It has comforted people down the centuries. Music still comforts, encourages, inspires, relaxes, stimulates. What a God-given gift it is, Lord!

I can only marvel, Lord, when I hear a symphony. The range of music, the variation in movements, the complexity of the arrangements are beyond my understanding. How could one man write these myriads of notes down, Lord? How could one mind conceive such combinations of notes and instruments? And how can one man or woman conductor so take it all in that they can create the magnificence of a great symphony? It is all beyond my comprehension, Lord, but it moves me greatly.

Nor does it surprise me, Lord, that music is therapeutic and, in skilled hands, can minister to those whom mere words cannot reach. Bless those, O Lord, who work in music therapy. Especially be with those who use music to help with problem children.

But tonight is for me, Lord. That I can go, after a busy, stressful day, and just listen to great music is heaven indeed. Be it Beethoven or Bach, Mozart or Mendlesohn, Brahms or Britten! "The world is filled with the grandeur of God" said e.e. cummings, Lord, and nowhere do I sense it more than in the wonderful world of musical composition.

In Jesus' name, Amen.

(12) After an evening at the cinema

There are times, O God, when it is right to escape for a little while from the trials, troubles and tensions of life in this modern world. And that I have done this evening when I chose to let myself be taken into a world of fantasy and fiction in the cinema. I deliberately did not choose to see anything focussed on violence or sex, Lord. I sought only a story of happiness and normality, a tale of family love and togetherness, a story with a happy ending.

Not all stories in the real world, Lord, have happy endings. The day's broadcast news is full of violence, war, murder, rape and abuse. I know that that is the world to which I shall return in two hours time, but that permissible escape from reality can be for my good, if I use it sensibly. Having done that tonight, for the pleasure of the evening, Lord, I give you thanks.

Perhaps, Lord, in that scenario, I see a picture of life itself. Retreat and return represent an understanding of the best way to cope with life. There are times, Lord, when I must escape for a period, as Jesus did so often, to be with you, O God, in order to gain renewal and strength, but it is not done for its own sake, Lord. It is always undertaken with a view to a return to the world.

I see this clearly, Lord, as I recall the life and work of the great Scottish innovator George MacLeod. In his vision of the Iona Community, he put together the concepts of retreat and return in a living scheme. Clergy would "retreat" for a period to the sacred island of Iona, not to do nothing, but, physically, to work on the rebuilding of the Abbey there, while in leisure time they would meet for fellowship, reflection and worship, thus spiritually "restoring their souls".

My "retreat" has been on a lesser scale, and for a more trivial reason, Lord, but, even so, I return relaxed and strengthened and a little more ready to wrestle with life in this world. For this, accept my gratitude, Lord.

Through Jesus Christ, my Lord, Amen.

(13) In the days of my youth

For the ability to walk far, run fast, jump high, play hard, all the things that I can do when I am young, I give you heartfelt thanks, O God. These are the years that I must treasure, for only when they have gone, Lord, will I fully appreciate them. So let me use them to the full in exercise and training, in sports and games, in contest and tournament, and in competitive engagement. But these too are the learning years when, as a result of intense study and challenging examinations, I will be equipped for life. How good it is to be young, Lord! How worthwhile are these years of preparation for living!

I realise too, O God, that I am maturing not only physically but emotionally, that physical change brings emotional strains. May any involvement in loving relationships that I have be unselfish, genuine, sensitive and caring. May I never treat anyone, Lord, as a means to my satisfaction but always look on others as beings created in your image. Then will my attitudes to others be those of respect, honesty and openness.

It is not easy, Lord, in these early, carefree years to have the sense of responsibility that experience brings, or to appreciate the weight of suffering that affects so many people. I therefore pray diligently for the grace of perceptiveness so that I can understand when other people have pain and be sympathetic to others' needs. And in enjoying the days of my youth, Lord, may I give others enjoyment too.

This prayer, I ask, in Jesus' name, Amen.

(14) In mid-life

O God, I come to you, facing the stress of middle years. As I reflect, in your presence, on the years that are past, mixed feelings struggle within me. In all honesty, Lord, there are some things that I have achieved, some aims that I have met, some minor successes that are on file. But there are too the failures that need to be looked at, the times when I fell short of my ideals; where, perhaps, I let myself or my family down; where hopes were not fulfilled.

"All have sinned and come short of the glory of God". "There is none righteous, no, not one". I read these statements in your Word, O God, and I know that they include me. To err is alas all too human. But there have been needless failings, careless acts, irrational thoughts and unwise decisions. If such failings are mine, I seek your forgiveness.

As I turn my thoughts to the years, be they many or few, that lie ahead of me, I renew my commitment to "love you, my God, with heart and soul and mind are strength" and "my neighbour as myself". Grant me the ability to sympathise with those in need, those who grieve, and the empathy to understand their weaknesses and failures. Make mine the listening ear and the tender heart.

O God, the years are there to be shaped and fashioned by me, but may that process always be effected within your providential care. May I be considerate of others and conscious of the need to do your will. And may my ability to fulfil these obligations bring me added blessings.

In Jesus' name, Amen.

(15) On returning from holiday

For the break from the daily round that I have enjoyed, I give you thanks, O God. To be able to set aside the pressures of work, the tediousness of routine, the demands of self-employment in order to enjoy relaxation, refreshment and renewal is one of life's true blessings. That such a benefit has come my way prompts me to praise again your providential care and your unfailing love.

The relationship between work and rest is enshrined, O God, in the story of creation. It tells of six days of labour and one of rest. You "rested from your labours", the Good Book says. Help us to learn from your example the inherent value there is in respite from effort, a respite that creates new zest for life, that provides the energy we need to serve others, that produces a zeal for your work and the gifts and graces needed to bring that work to fruition… patience, persistence and power.

When a time of holiday comes, Lord, enable us to appreciate anew, the open air, the heavens which declare your glory and the wonder of your world. Give us minds that are open to new insights, hearts that respond to beauty, a thirst for greater knowledge and the enthusiasm to welcome new approaches to living. May we, in all our encounters with people, manifest humility, dignity and openness, a readiness to appreciate other cultures while always properly representing our own.

So may we rejoice to be alive, Lord, in this your wonderful world.

Through Jesus Christ, our Lord, Amen.

(16) On renewing acquaintance

I approach this day with excitement, Lord, for I am to see again a friend long separated from me. We have been kept apart not by choice but by circumstance. I have missed my friend, with whom, in my younger days, I shared so much… school days, teenage years, our early married lives… until business needs took that valued friend to faraway places. Today, Lord, for the first time in years, we will, if you so will it, meet again.

How important, Lord, are those friendships formed when we are young. Shared interests, shared laughter, shared secrets… they called us "soul mates", Lord, and so we were. We had an intimacy born of mutual trust, an empathy, the product of mutual understanding. We supported each other through happy school days, encouraged each other through the challenging years of university and college, rejoiced in each others' success, and wished each other well when we chose our partners. Then it all changed and the separation years took over. Until today, Lord.

Yet, perhaps not unsurprisingly, Lord, I feel apprehensive. Will I recognise my friend of bygone years? Not just physically but spiritually? Have we held on to the wonderful mutuality that we had? Will conversation be easy? Shall we find much or indeed anything in common, Lord? So, as the hours before our reunion count slowly down, I wait and I wonder, and I even tremble, Lord.

At last it has happened, Lord. We met. We hugged. We looked at each other. We cried. It was as if we had never been apart. It was difficult for either of us to believe it, but to deny it was impossible. We were as one. We were reunited, totally, completely.

What a glorious gift is friendship, Lord!

Thanks be to God, Amen.

Section 2: 17- 39

In dark and dismal days

(17) At the end of a bad day

This, O God, has been a bad day. I set out with good intensions, positive plans, eager hopes, but I come to this time of evening prayer, disappointed, dejected and feeling defeated, Lord. And yet I don't really know why things just did not go well. I always seek to be positive, Lord. I look for good in people. I believe that life is what we make it. But from the beginning of the day to its end, things seemed to go wrong. And I wonder why. Did I make mistakes? Did I handle people insensitively?

Lord, help me to think clearly on these things. I know I have a tendency to ride rough shod over other people, convinced that I have the answers to problems and the ability to provide them. Is this a confidence that slips over the border into arrogance? Am I unwilling to listen, to take on board other approaches, other ideas? Am I unable to "hear" people, Lord, when they are quietly telling me that I am wrong? If any of these things are true, Lord, grant me the grace to respond positively and graciously.

This day is done, Lord, and I cannot change the errors I have made. Rather prepare me to face tomorrow with a determination to ensure it is a good and useful day. Its success or failure will not be decided by mythical spirits intent on doing me ill, but by the way I handle people and projects, frame policies and initiate action. Give me then, Lord, a clear mind, a wise discretion, a willingness to cooperate and a proper determination to succeed in whatever I set out to do. And if a bad day today has helped me to frame a better tomorrow, may I be truly thankful, Lord.

In Jesus' name, Amen.

(18) When we receive disappointments

I was looking forward to today, Lord, for the diary tells me a friend was due to come in for a cup of tea and a chat. I arranged the day around this and set out the work I had to do before she came. Now, just before she is due, Lord, she has rung to say that she cannot come. I understand the reason but, Lord, I feel considerable disappointment. I am also struggling against feelings of resentment, Lord.

Is it wrong for me to be annoyed, Lord? Am I upset because I feel I have been made of secondary importance to my friend's needs? Why did she not tell me earlier that she could not come and I would not have rushed my own work as I did? Or am I being just small-minded, putting myself first?

Life consists of important things, Lord, and a host of trivial things. In what category does this matter fall, Lord? This is a trivial matter, Lord, and I have to be gracious enough to accept it in that spirit. For her, what she had to do was urgent and I should appreciate that that was so. Now having been given time I did not expect to have, I should redeem it and see it as opportunity.

O God, help me to learn from this situation the need for tolerance and trust, tolerance of the right of somebody to make decisions disappointing to me, trust in the integrity of my friend. May there be a broadness of mind in my attitude to all life's circumstances and situations. May I never try to live as if I am the centre of the world.

Through Jesus Christ, my Lord, Amen.

(19) Facing the mystery of suffering

One hundred and fifty thousand dead in an earthquake. Thousands lost when a terrifying tsunami thunders over seaside villages. A little child is killed on a footpath when a speeding car runs out of control. One close friend decimated by dementia: another critically ill with cancer. O God, how can these things be? How can they be allowed to happen if you really are a God of unfailing love?

Questions like these exercise and agonise my mind, Lord. Such tragedy! Such unfairness! Such cruel situations! And so often it seems to be good people who suffer so, while, unruffled and unharmed, the violent and the vile go on their way, rejoicing. How can I contain such mystery, Lord? How can I explain these things? How can I defend the faith I proclaim so confidently when it seems to centre on an absent God?

And yet, at the very centre of my faith, I face the same dilemma. Looking to Jesus, there is the one who did no sin, yet he was nailed to a cross. Was that fair, O God? Why should that happen, Lord?

Somehow, in ways beyond my comprehension, we are saved through suffering, Jesus' suffering. "He died that we may be forgiven" we sing, Lord. "He died to make us good". Somehow, through an act as cruel as crucifixion, "love's redeeming work is done".

I do not understand, Lord, but, in faith, I believe. I am convinced that your will for us is our good. I therefore leave all these mysteries in your hands.

In Jesus' name, Amen.

(20) "When sadness fills my mind"

"When sadness fills my mind, a solace here I find". The lines of an old hymn are running through my mind, Lord. I wonder why. Perhaps the answer is in the telephone message awaiting me on my return this afternoon, Lord. It was to let me know that a dear friend has died. The news is sad indeed, very sad.

I have known this friend over many years, Lord, but we had very little actual physical contact. There was however a profound intuitive bond between us, never verbally expressed, but inwardly acknowledged on both sides. Respect and affection were its main ingredients, Lord.

I have known for some three years or so that my dear friend was very ill and undergoing long-term treatment. For her recovery, I have consistently prayed. It seemed so unfair that such a good person, one of the finest folk I have ever known, should suffer so.

As I think of the husband, mother and sons that she leaves, so my thoughts are with all whose minds are filled with sadness this day. Many will have lost dear friends. Others will be sad for other reasons. Have you perhaps failed to achieve targets you set, and are very disappointed as a result? Have you, yet again, fallen victim to the sins that "made (Jesus) mourn?" Have you been let down by someone you trusted?

O God, whatever be the grounds of my sadness, today, I seek solace in your words of comfort, your promised forgiveness, your overarching providence. There is so much that I do not understand, Lord, but there is also the ongoing faith that I do have. May I therefore cease to be "restless… until I rest in you".

Through Jesus Christ, my Lord, Amen.

(21) When someone has let me down

I face this day with resentment and bitterness, O God. I have been let down, Lord. I had infinite trust in my colleague, whom I have known for many years, but suddenly, for no good reason, he has left me stranded. The shock is hard to bear, Lord, for I believe in people.

The project we planned had such possibilities, Lord. It would have benefitted our families, blessed our future, secured our businesses. But, in a moment, all this has disappeared. Tempted by the prospect of another project, with some other partner, for greater gain, my colleague has withdrawn his investment and in so doing, he has endangered my future, crippled my finances, hurt my family and left me distraught with anxiety. Have I not the right to feel bitter, Lord?

Betrayal, for this is what my friend has done to me, Lord, is something that is hard to bear. It destroys confidence in people. It creates the kind of bitterness I feel today, Lord. It conditions future relationships, making one wary of trusting anyone again. How can I banish these negative feelings, which I feel are wholly foreign to my faith, Lord?

I find help, Lord, looking to the life of Jesus, for he was betrayed, let down by one who called him Master, delivered to hostile authorities by the one who would identify him by giving him a kiss. But the Lord Jesus showed no bitterness, Lord, just sorrow and sadness for the one who had betrayed him.

Help me, O God, in this my difficult hour, to try to follow the example of my Lord.

Through Jesus Christ, my Lord, Amen.

(22) When you suffer loss

I give you thanks, O God, that when Jesus heard that his friend, Lazarus, had died, he wept. That tells me that you understand how I feel now that I have suffered a great personal loss. Your Word assures us that, in the light of Jesus' resurrection, "death has no more dominion over us". Deep down, I accept that truth but, here and now, when someone I greatly loved has died, I struggle to hold on to that belief. Death feels so final. Yesterday my loved one was here with me; today she has gone from me, if not in memory, in terms of her physical presence. And that, Lord, is hard to bear.

Death is, paradoxically, part of life. It comes, at least in my case, Lord, after many years of happy togetherness. I will, no doubt (as I believe), in time ease into acceptance of my loved one's death and be grateful for the good memories. But this loss has come in middle life, with fearful suddenness. Give me then, good Lord, time to grieve and the space to find some inner peace. But that will not be easy, Lord. Be patient with my frailty. Be understanding of my tears. Be gentle with me, when I am tempted to self-pity. And when feelings of grief suddenly overwhelm me, be "God with me".

"I believe in the resurrection and the life". That is my conviction, Lord, and in it, I rejoice. But comfort and strengthen me as I struggle to come to terms with the reality to which I have to become accustomed and with which I must make friends. Transform my loneliness into a creative solitude through which I recover my sense of peace.

In Jesus' name, Amen.

(23) When depressed

The sunshine of yesterday has gone, Lord. Dark clouds of depression have engulfed me. Just why this has happened, I do not know. But of the reality of this dark mood, I have no doubt. Lord, save me.

"When I awake" said the Psalmist, "I am still with you". But it does not feel like that today, Lord. I just feel so alone, so vulnerable, so isolated. Irrational fears surge through my mind. Dread of the unknown future begins to overwhelm me. I try hard to overcome negative feelings, Lord, but it is to no avail. With all the strength of will I can muster, I cannot lighten this darkness.

That depression is at its worst in the early hours of the day, I have, from experience, long known, Lord, but, from time to time, it still brings me strain and stress, damages my faith and destroys hope.

"Trust in the Lord with all your heart and do not lean on your own understanding" the Good Book says. How true this is, Lord. On myself, I cannot depend. Waiting on you, I must look outside myself for help, seeking the grace offered in your unfailing love. It is, I remind myself again, not my grasp of you that matters but your grasp of me, Lord.

And so, in disciplined silence, I wait on you now, Lord, and as I do this, I seem to hear you telling me to think of others' needs, not just my own. There is a selfishness that manifests itself in wallowing in one's own unhappiness. I hear you saying that the way to peace is through serving others.

I thank you, Lord, for gently leading me towards proportion and perspective. Lifted up in mind and mood, I am now more ready to face this day.

Through Jesus Christ, my Lord, Amen.

(24) When over-worked

How tired and weary I feel tonight, Lord. The day has been so stressful. Some people have been so demanding. Some work has been left undone. I end the day, Lord, feeling over-worked, depleted, strained. I try so hard to fulfil my responsibilities, achieve my goals and meet my targets, but today, Lord, it was all too much. And I feel disappointed, dissatisfied with myself, devoid of energy and defeated.

In all my working life, I have tried to do my best, Lord, to fulfil expectations, both those of myself and of others. I have been consistent in my application, enthusiastic in the pursuit of all I am asked to do, energetic in my efforts to accomplish my objectives. But tonight, Lord, I have reached something of a crisis. I need perspective, Lord, and refreshment too.

"Seek first the Kingdom of God and its righteousness" Jesus says "and other things will be added to you". I reflect on these words, Lord, and try to apply them to my motivation and application. As I think on these things, I feel that Jesus did not have in mind the *amount* of time to be allocated to this and to that. I suspect he was talking of *proportion*, about the way we look at life, Lord. And maybe that is where I am going wrong, Lord. Not intentionally, but in reality, I am letting the "other things", that is the worldly, material things I have to do, so consume me that I am spiritually drained.

Let me be still, O Lord, this night and approach tomorrow and the work I have to do, with a fresh outlook. I must still do my work fully and faithfully, but I must control it, not let it control me. And whatever I am doing, may I do it "as unto the Lord", with graciousness and grace.

I ask this in Jesus' name, Amen.

(25) When passing through "the dark night"

While saints and mystics have experienced the "dark night of the soul", lesser Christians, like me, Lord, have suffered the darkness too. Desolate, in despair, I feel abandoned by you, O God, bereft of the Spirit and utterly alone. Yet in my loneliness, I do not seek the company of people, even close friends or the family. I look only to wallowing in my unhappiness, drifting into self-pity, avoiding contact with the world. My creativity has gone. I cannot write and do not want to read. Neither radio or television can draw me away from my self-centredness, my problems, my sins. What abject misery this is, Lord!

Why have I reached this desperate condition, Lord? I look for reasons but do not learn much. I am aware that I have been going downhill for some time, withdrawing more and more from life, the world and people. I have ceased to answer the phone, open correspondence, go to the door when the bell rings. I wait in hope for bed-time, though I know that I will not sleep and listen for the dawn, though I know I shall not want to get up. This, Lord, is not life. It is but empty existence. And such darkness, Lord.

Despite my losing faith, I hold on to the knowledge that your grasp of me, Lord, will hold and that, given time, you will draw me back with the cords of love. Meantime, for every glimpse of light in the darkness, I thank you as I do for every tiny movement I may make towards reality and perspective. The time will come when I shall live again. Give me the patience to wait for your time of salvation to come. And when that comes, help me to seize the moment of potential resurrection.

Through Jesus Christ, my Lord, Amen.

(26) In a time of doubt

My faith is wavering, Lord. I thought my faith was sure and steadfast, but here and now, I am uncertain and unsure.

Why is this, Lord? Is it because I am physically tired? Am I mentally weary, struggling against the perceived injustice of "the slings and arrows of outrageous fortune?" I cannot tell, Lord, but at this moment, I just do not feel I know whom I have believed, nor am I persuaded that you, O God, can do those things which I long for you to do.

Like Simon Peter on the Sea of Galilee, I feel that I am sinking, Lord. Like Thomas, doubting Thomas, my mind yearns for some proof of your existence and your power. I am tempted to become the fool who says there is no God. What or who can save me from this uncomfortable doubt and restore my sense of peace? Yet, in my heart, I know it is not you who have let go of me. I have lost my grasp of you.

Grant me the courage to wait on you in the stillness, so that I may recover some feeling of confidence in your providential care and find it possible to believe anew that you are the God who simply will not let us go.

Draw me to you with the cords of love. Help me to realise that I do not need to understand everything in order to recover my faith.

It is your grasp of me, Lord, that matters. I know that you will give me back my peace.

I make this plea through Jesus Christ, my Lord.

(27) In the depths of despair

O God, I feel so low. Your servant, Jacob, once cried out in mental agony when suffering repeated losses: "All these things are against me". That is how I feel, Lord, today.

I seem to be battered by hostile circumstances. One thing after another goes completely wrong. One friend after another falls ill, has an accident. Others I know have extreme worries, are in desperate circumstances. And I seem to suffer one bereavement after another. Sometimes, indeed all too often, the cause is cancer. Sometimes a heart attack. Sometimes Alzheimer's Disease. Some may be advanced in years, but some are only in mid-life. Sometimes, and it is so sad, Lord, it is a little child. No matter how hard I try to be positive, forward-looking, serene, I struggle in vain. I fight against gloom, despair, even desolation, but little success comes. How do I overcome this darkness, Lord?

It is my faith, O God, that you never leave us or forsake us. Are you still there in the darkness, Lord? I believe you are; that because "darkness and light are both alike to you", it is in the darkness, I catch a glimpse of you, the light. Truly the darkest hour is just before your dawn.

Grant me the courage to believe that you are always "God with us", God with me, not least when I am in greatest despair. Break through the darkness, O God, and take me towards the light.

In Jesus' name, Amen.

(28) "When in the night, I sleepless lie…"

O God, how blessed is the gift of sleep, but how awful when it will just not come. Last night was one such night, Lord, and today I feel totally washed out.

It was a trying day yesterday, Lord. Nothing went according to plan. News of family difficulties upset me and I lay down to rest, far too late, mind churning, unhappy, confused. It was no use, Lord. I tossed and turned, ever seeking some way to sleep, but it was all in vain. The hours ticked slowly by until, at last, I dropped off with only a short time until the dawn and harsh reality again.

In the past, I have often drawn help from Jesus' encouraging words, and with those comforting words in the forefront of my mind, I have faced and overcome frightening situations. But, although I said those words: "Let not your heart be troubled, neither let it be afraid" many times, Lord, my mind found no stillness, my heart knew no peace.

But I have learned a little, Lord, through this hard lesson. It is not for you to solve my problems for me. It is for me to let you be with me when they come. You are the God who, your Psalmist says, "neither slumbers nor sleeps", so that waking, failing to sleep or sleeping, you are always there. Help me so absorb this truth that, "when in the night I sleepless lie", I can draw on this assurance and, leaving all things in your hands, find peace. For, as the Psalmist tells me again, Lord, "When I awake, I am still with you".

In Jesus' name, Amen.

(29) When in severe pain

How long, O God, am I to suffer so? I am living with arthritic pain and have so lived for years now, Lord. How difficult it is to cope with it! My limbs are sore, my fingers hurt. It all makes life so complicated for me, Lord. I cannot grip anything firmly or safely. My walking speed is low. My movement laboured. And my physical problems place burdens on others, something that concerns me greatly. How long, Lord, will I have to live with this burden? Will I ever be free from pain, Lord?

I give you thanks, Lord, for the wonders of modern medicine and for medication that can dull pain down, thus giving me some freedom from suffering. I am grateful for that, Lord.

Deep in my heart is a profound belief in the healing power of Jesus. It is my conviction, O God, that Jesus heals today, that if you so will it, miracles can take place. But that is in your hands, O God, and I leave it there in faith. What I must do is be faithful in prayer, but always in the context of "Your will be done".

For now, Lord, grant me the patience I need to bear the pain, the determination to keep on the move and the will to overcome limitations and inconvenience. May I always move forward boldly and bravely, conscious of your presence and committed to seeking your purpose for me. In times of pain, enable me to maintain the grace of cheerfulness. Concentrate my concern on others, rather than on myself and my problems. And in everything may I be able to give thanks.

And this I ask through Jesus Christ, my Lord, Amen.

(30) When seriously ill

O God, I come to you, knowing I am ill with recovery not yet in sight. The outlook, at present, is poor, Lord and the pain is great. The crisis point in my illness has not yet been reached and I am in mental disarray. I cannot rest, I cannot eat, I cannot sleep, I am weak in body and depressed in spirit, Lord. In compassion, hear my prayer.

I give you thanks, Lord, for the miracles of modern medicine. I entrust myself to professional care. I am grateful for the medication that will easy my pain, the drugs that will help me sleep and the treatments available to me. I know I should not be "troubled or afraid", but I confess that my mind is restless and ill at ease. My mind will be restless until it rests in you. Therefore, in my deep need, I wait upon you now.

I thank you for those who lovingly care for me, for the friends who want to visit me. I pray, Lord, that they may have an understanding of where I am and what I do not need. Help me to set aside negative feelings about my illness, and resentment, perhaps, at "this happening to me".

Now, O God, is the time to bring into action the faith I claim to have had for so long. Help me to be at peace and able to reflect on "Jesus and his love". Make real for me the wonder of the healing power that comes from you. Give me the faith I need now, the hope that comes from that faith, and the peace that is born of hope. So may I leave all things in your care, O Lord, and feel that all will yet be truly well.

I ask this in Jesus' name, Amen.

(31) When harshly criticised

How moving, O God, is the silence of dignity demonstrated by Jesus before his accusers. I read in your Word that, faced with harsh and wholly unfair criticism from those who claimed he was guilty of, according to some, blasphemy, according to others, sedition, "Jesus answered them nothing". That surely was the perfect answer to such groundless accusations; a dignified silence.

I ponder this passage deeply today, Lord. Because I am in a public position, I am subject to criticism. When therefore issues arise that demand clear decisions in controversial situations, and I have to make a stand on a principle, inevitably there are those who rail against me. I accept this, Lord, as inherent in my professional role, but I find it hard when critics question my integrity and savage my character. The human side of me wants to answer back, Lord, to defend my position and my honour. Perhaps, Lord, I need to learn from Jesus and realise that the best answer to unjust criticism is to say nothing.

To do this, Lord, requires a "plenitude of grace". It is our human instinct to want to respond on the basis of the formula "an eye for an eye and a tooth for a tooth". That is a normal human response, Lord. The words of Jesus are, however, clear. We are not to resist evil, but rather to do good to those who hate us. The silence of dignity is a much better response, as Jesus demonstrated so clearly.

So, at all times and in whatever circumstances, including those of harsh and unjust criticism, may my walk be "close with God, calm and serene my frame".

Through Jesus Christ, my Lord, Amen.

(32) When a relationship ends

O God, I bring to you a broken heart. Someone I love has brought their relationship with me to an end. I did not see this coming, Lord. All seemed to be well between us. There have been no arguments or disagreements. No hint of what has gone wrong has been conveyed to me. Yet all of a sudden, I learn, to my distress, that there is someone else of whom I must take account. I am distraught, Lord.

Where two people have a loving relationship and mutual devotion has marked every stage of it, confidence and trust are endemic. I have not, therefore, thought of any situation arising that could endanger what I believed we both held dear. But the unthinkable has come to pass, Lord. For the one I love, there is now someone else.

It is difficult, Lord, to prevent feelings of bitterness and resentment flooding my mind. I have given so much of myself to the one I thought of as my partner for all time. And now, I am left on my own. It does not feel fair, Lord. It is not fair.

I must, O Lord, "take this to the Lord in prayer", but I do so knowing my heart is broken and my anger real. I seek refuge in self-pity and, feeling sorry for myself, have little room for concern for others and certainly for the one who has invaded our loving world.

O God, my very soul is at risk. I must somehow deal firmly with the negative feelings filling my mind and hurting my feelings. I therefore come to you in my emotional agony and say "Be still, my soul".

Through Jesus Christ, my Lord, Amen.

(33) When broken-hearted

My heart is breaking, Lord. For news has come which I can hardly believe. One dear to me has been arrested, Lord. On a serious charge. Driving home, after unwisely accepting a social drink, he has had an accident as a result of which a cyclist he hit, in the dark, has died. Released on bail, he will be in court soon and, having allegedly driven without due care and attention, he will surely go to jail. He is, Lord, no criminal in the accepted sense. He has never been in trouble before but, combining foolishness and carelessness, he is now held responsible for the death of a young man.

For the family of the dead man, Lord, my heart bleeds. That is tragedy indeed, but what am I to think of my friend, Lord, in the circumstances in which he finds himself now? His wife is distraught too, distraught at the suffering he has caused, but distraught also over the consequences of what he has done. It is heart-breaking, Lord.

There is no point in ranting and raging at my friend, however great the wrong he has done. He knows all too well the guilt he feels and the punishment he deserves. Rightly or wrongly, Lord, I am drawn to offer, not harsh criticism, but sympathetic support. There, but for the grace of God…

It is not for me, or anyone else, Lord to condone the foolishness that leads to such a disaster, but surely, here and now, I must combine judgement with mercy and leave it to the appropriate authorities to see that justice is done. I must stand by my friend in this tragedy for, for him, it is his tragedy too. And when he has paid the penalty that society demands, I must help him back towards the normality he may never fully regain.

In Jesus' name, Amen.

(34) On suffering rejection

I end this day, O God, in sadness. I had pinned my hopes on the success of a writing project, but what I submitted has been, to my great disappointment, rejected.

O God, I bring this situation to the throne of grace. Grant me, I pray, the ability to retain perspective and the will to start again. The failure may be my fault. I perhaps did not consider others' interests and needs. It may be that I was not objective enough about what I had written. Nor will I be the first, Lord to receive a rejection. Learn from it I must. Give me the grace to do that, Lord.

That others have not seen and appreciated the value of what I have done, Lord, must not lead me to think that I have no talent. I believe that you have given me gifts, and these I must develop through hard work, self-criticism and listening to advice. Let me then, Lord, move on to tomorrow and take up afresh the challenge to succeed. Keep me humble in attitude, Lord, strong in self-belief, sensitive to new knowledge and ready to learn from others of greater experience.

Bless the tomorrow to which I now turn, and strengthened by my faith and calling, help me to create something of value, something of true worth, Lord. Prevent me from thinking always in terms of commercial gain, but keep me realistic in terms of my human needs, so that what feels like the tragedy of today may be honed into the triumph of tomorrow, to my innate satisfaction and, at the same time, to your glory.

Through Jesus Christ, my Lord.

(35) If you live alone

It is my lot, Lord, to live alone. The loss of a partner, family circumstances, even choice, may contribute to my situation. However that may be, help me to say, as your servant Paul did: "I have learned to find contentment, whatever my circumstances".

To be on one's own, Lord, can bring about the blessing of solitude or the curse of loneliness. Safeguard me from that latter fate. Make me grateful for the gift of family and friends. Do not let me slip into increasing bitterness over the misfortunes and injustices of life as contributors to my loneliness. It would be better, Lord, if I could welcome the benefits of being alone, for benefits there can be if I look for them.

When, resentfully, because I am weary with much of life, I am tempted to seek isolation, give me the will to mix with others. Help me to think of their needs rather than engage in the selfishness of self-pity. Make real for me the great truth that "perfect love casts out fear", that life is best lived in the service of others; that caring for those less fortunate than I am, I will never be lonely.

For the blessing of the solitude which being on my own gives me, I give you thanks, Lord. I am encouraged by Jesus, who so deliberately sought solitude. Through that strengthening silence he found the ability to engage with life and people all the more. I thank you, too, O God, for the solitude that enables me to meditate on your Word and brings me nearer to him of whom, with Thomas, I will say: "My Lord and my God".

And this I ask through Jesus Christ, my Lord, Amen.

(36) When you are in debt

O God, I come to you deeply in trouble, all of it my own making. I am in debt, Lord, deeply in debt. I have lived beyond my means, made foolish decisions and greedily fed my selfish desires. Contrary to your command, I have coveted what others had. I have been enticed into spending by the attractiveness of material things. Blindly, I have gone on and on, borrowing what I could not repay, leaning on credit when lusting after luxuries. For these faults, indeed sins, and the situation into which they have led me, I alone am to blame, Lord.

It says in the Psalms, Lord, of those who are at their wits end, that they "cry to the Lord". But what right have I, the sole author of my troubles, to ask you to bail me out? But you are, according to my faith, a God of unfailing love, ever ready to forgive those who return to you, in abject humility and sincere penitence. I believe that, for it is your promise, that forgiveness will be mine, but with the responsibility on me to put right whatever wrongs I have done, and to express sorrow to any who have been hurt by my irresponsibility.

I know too, Lord, that I must find the self-discipline that I have lacked and exercise the control that I now seriously need. You helping me, O God, I can do this. I must rein in my longing for possessions and deny selfish lusting after this world's goods. I must no longer, under any circumstances, a borrower be. Grant me the strength of will to embrace this demanding task in humility, with discipline and a clear head.

In Jesus' name, Amen.

(37) On hearing of a natural disaster

O God, I am distraught this day. As I watch the "breaking news" of a great disaster, an earthquake, in the Far East, I am appalled at the level of the destruction, at the immensity of the loss of life, at the number of the injured. How can I begin to compute the cost in pain and tears of (it is said) over one hundred thousand dead and thousands more missing? "Where is your God of love?", our enemies will say. "Where is he?" I too must ask, in desperation, Lord.

What a dilemma of faith such events bring about. How difficult it is to explain, or explain away such natural disasters and the destruction that they bring. It cannot be, Lord, that this is corporate punishment for sins committed. Why should the population of one country suffer so? Are we not all sinners across the globe? As Jesus said, as recorded in your Word, Lord, were the people on whom the tower of Siloam fell the only sinners, and those who escaped sinless? No, Lord, it cannot be. Disaster falls indiscriminately on all.

I watch these pictures of destruction and despair with incredulity, Lord, and with judgement suspended. There is an element of mystery in global suffering beyond my understanding, Lord. I can only pray for every one of them, caught up in such cataclysmic tragedy as I do for those who rush to minister to them.

It is with that faith that I pray today for that countless, unnumbered host, caught up in this inexplicable mystery, a mass of unknown people, yet each one a "child of God", a child of yours. In your compassion, be with each one of them, Lord.

In Jesus' name, Amen.

(38) In a time of war

"You shall hear of wars and rumours of wars" said your servant, James. And so we do, Lord. Will conflicts and battles never end?

The dreaded news some family does not want is, alas, delivered daily. A roadside bomb, a helicopter crash, "friendly fire". "The family have been informed". The causes of a loved one's death may vary, but the agony never ends.

The Great War, The Second World War, The Falklands, Iraq, Afghanistan… the litany of war goes on and on. Will it never cease, Lord?

"From where do wars and fightings come?" James goes on to ask. He answers his own question, Lord. "From within you. You kill and covet…" For what reason do men and women resort to arms? Moral reasons? The response to terrorism? The politics of power? Ideology? Oil?

We only see through a glass darkly, Lord. And almost always from our own point of view. But some other way needs to be found, Lord, lest in seeking to destroy others, we destroy ourselves. Deep divisions in a nuclear age are dangerous indeed. How desperately we must try to find other solutions to the problems between competing powers.

O Lord, our God, come forward and bless every constructive effort to make peace. Strengthen and bless the United Nations Organisation. Encourage universally the ministry of reconciliation. Above all, change the hearts and minds of those who see in violence the only means of change.

Give peace in my time, O Lord.

In Jesus' name, Amen.

(39) When someone takes their life

I come to you this night, O God, deeply distressed. Someone I know and greatly respect has taken his life. It all happened as it was intended to happen, after careful planning and with considerable forethought, Lord, and yet it took family and friends by surprise. Relations had not been aware of an existing or impending crisis. Friends had not suspected that a life of unhappiness and perhaps desperation was being lived out among them. It was with a heavy heart I heard the news, Lord. He alone, who took his life, knows why he did it.

In one way, I am angry, Lord, that this man, in middle life, did what he did without letting me or others know he was in mortal emotional pain. No chance to help was allowed to anyone. But then again, I feel distraught as I ponder the stress he must have felt, for extreme stress there must have been within him to bring about this death. Was it lack of money? Loss of self-worth? A sense of helplessness about the present, whatever that present might be? A feeling of hopelessness about life itself?

And so our mingled feelings of anger, guilt and sympathy stumble on; anger because we were not given the chance to help, guilt that we may, in some way, have let him down, sympathy as we realise the depths of anguish through which he must have gone. I do not know, nor can I tell, what inner pain he had to bear. I can only commit this man to your unfailing love and understanding, Lord. You alone will know the secrets that led to this tragedy so you alone will understand.

Through Jesus Christ, my Lord, Amen.

Section 3

Sundry Occasions: 40-64

(40) On getting up

Thank you for the dawn of this new day, O God. It comes with hope, with expectation, with eager anticipation. It presents a page in my history, Lord, waiting to be written. May I grasp this opportunity to share in creation, Lord. May I pursue ideals, be ready to take creative risks, make sound decisions and, going forward in faith, achieve something of value this day. Lord, bless this day and may it be to your glory.

"The daily round, the common task", I sang on Sunday "will furnish all we ought to ask". O God, help me to carry out the routine duties of this day with efficiency, care and cheerfulness. In my relationships with the family, Lord, make me available, helpful and sensitive to need. In my encounters with people, Lord, may I always be gracious and thoughtful, diligent in caring, devoted to helping. But grant me too, O Lord, the opportunity to be alone and quiet, giving time to the things of the Spirit, nurturing my faith. So may I reach the end of the day, Lord, able to look back in gratitude for blessings received.

O God, let my attitude to each day be determined by your servant, James, who in his New Testament letter lays down exactly what that daily attitude must be. He takes to task those who simply say "Tomorrow I will do this and that". Rightly he tells us, Lord, that I should always say, whether in words or in my heart: "If the Lord wills it, I shall do this and that". I thank you Lord for this word. It constantly reminds me of the whole context of my life in Christ.

I ask this prayer through Jesus Christ, my Lord, Amen.

(41) Before a medical appointment

"Neither be troubled or afraid!" How grateful I am so often, O God, for these words of Jesus to his disciples. I know the particular circumstances for which they were uttered, Lord, but I feel Jesus would understand it if they were applied to many other situations that we face in life. They helped me through serious circumstances that I have had to face in my past. I call on them today as I face the anxiety of a medical appointment. It is the fear of the unknown that is so difficult, Lord. It is not easy to be without fear at such times. Help me to be untroubled and unafraid, Lord.

Whatever poses a threat to our future inevitably brings anxiety. What have the tests already done revealed, Lord? What will x-rays to be taken today show? Will there be procedures put in place that will be uncomfortable or painful? How active my imagination has become as it races through possibilities and probabilities, Lord! I know such flights into the unknown are foolish, but it is human to be both troubled and afraid and that I am, Lord.

I am struggling also to keep back worries about my future, Lord. If there is something seriously wrong, how will my life, my work, my family be affected? If I need surgery, how long will rehabilitation take? If I need intensive treatment, will I be able to cope? There is indeed much about which to be troubled and afraid, Lord.

"Drop thy still dews of quietness till all our strivings cease". The time has come to be still and remember that you are God, to cease these imaginary strivings and to be calm, to say again, in mantra-like repetition: "be neither troubled or afraid". Your continuing presence is your promised gift, Lord. Yes, I am now ready to be neither troubled or afraid.

In Jesus' name, Amen.

(42) When in hospital

I am ill at ease, Lord. I find myself unexpectedly in hospital, in unfamiliar surroundings, and with a sense of apprehension too, Lord. It was a sudden collapse that brought me here. Preliminary examinations led to a decision to admit me and here I am in a ward awaiting further investigation.

I have been blessed with many years of good health, Lord and for that I am grateful. But how easy it is to take good health for granted. What has happened to me, Lord... and I do not yet know what has gone wrong... brings uncertainty and insecurity. All this uncertainty is causing me feelings of dis-ease and I find I am yes, I have to admit it, afraid.

I am in good hands. I am in a place where everything is geared to helping me to be well: consultants at the top of their profession, doctors with years of training, nurses, many of them with long experience, equipment that is up-to-date, sophisticated drugs. All this must surely give me confidence, Lord. Over and above that, I ought to have an awareness of your over-arching care, the sense of a providence in which I most surely believe.

I have been x-rayed, scanned and closely examined. There is nothing seriously wrong. Shortly I shall be released to resume my normal life. But, O God, may I learn from this episode. May I never take for granted the blessing of good health. May I not forget to intercede for those engaged in healthcare, for they too are among the countless blessings for which we must constantly give thanks. In your divine generosity, Lord, you supply our needs. To you be the glory!

I ask all this in Jesus' name, Amen.

(43) Before an operation

"Be still and know that I am God". These words run through my mind as I face this day, O God. Repeatedly. For this is the day I have dreaded since I saw the specialist and learned that I must undergo surgery. It is my first experience of a major operation and it frightens me, Lord. How sincere my whispered prayer is! How greatly I need your stillness, Lord!

To fall asleep each night is an act of faith. To allow consciousness to slip away, deliberately, and pass eight hours in blissful unawareness is one of life's kindnesses, Lord, and for it, I am unceasingly grateful. To lose consciousness here in hospital in these circumstances is much more threatening and unnerving. What will happen to me while I am under the anaesthetic is beyond my knowledge. How I shall be when, in your providence, I come round, is a concern for me. I say again, as I lie, waiting to be "taken down", "Be still and know that I am God". My immediate future is in others' hands… and yours.

An hour has passed and slowly, Lord, I am beginning to regain consciousness. There is no sign of surgeon, anaesthetist or their assistants. Their work for me is done and they have moved on to care for someone else. I thank you for them all, Lord, as I do for the nurses now looking after me.

But more than all else, I thank you for the peace of mind you gave me, Lord, on my journey into the unknown.

Through Jesus Christ, my Lord, Amen.

(44) On sitting examinations

"Drop thy still dews of quietness till all our strivings cease". Lord, I quietly recite the words of John Greenleaf Whittier's hymn as I seek to be calm before today's crucial exams. I know, Lord, that my future welfare will be very much affected by the results I achieve, so the words of that hymn speak to me at this time when my mind is full and my nerves are taut. "Take from our souls the strain and stress" he goes on, and I repeat that plea for inner calm, over and over again. "Be still, my soul…" How I plead for that stillness now as I prepare to go to the exam room. I need a clear head and a serene heart. Grant me your peace, Lord.

In the past, exams have not been a great problem for me, Lord. I try to prepare well, to know my facts and to read the questions carefully to ensure I have understood what answers are being sought. But today, Lord, is somehow different. So much is at stake in this particular exam that I am facing it with reduced confidence.

It is therefore essential, Lord, that I find mental peace quickly and settle confidently to the task in hand. I must make a conscious effort to take control, wilfully to force myself to calm down and wait on you, Lord, asking for your help. I alone can sit the exam, but, in terms of my faith and belief, you are "God with us" in every situation, and so I can ask you, in Jesus' name, to be in that room with me. So let these exams now be faced with quiet confidence and a vibrant calm, believing this important episode is enfolded in the curtain of your loving care, Lord.

The time of testing is at hand, Lord. May I meet it confidently, your promise reverberating in my mind: "My peace I give to you".

Through Jesus Christ, my Lord, Amen.

(45) Before an important test

I face a test today, Lord. It is a day which I have anticipated with apprehension because my future depends on how I cope with it. I do not find such tests easy, Lord, but I know the importance of approaching them with as clear a head as possible. I must be in firm control of time so that I complete the test without creating extra tension. I must combine succinctness with adequate answers. I must rely on my ability, knowledge and the capacity I know I have for conciseness and accuracy. And, as with everything I do, I will go to this test, Lord, believing you are, as always, "God with us", not doing things for us, but energising us and strengthening us.

We live in a ruthless world where the pursuit of material things drives so many people on. The pressure to possess this world's goods is all around us, Lord. The need to have what others have can take us over. The sheer necessity of survival and helping one's family to survive and progress is a constant pressure on us. May I approach this test, not motivated by an unworthy competitiveness, Lord, but only by the desire to do the best that I can, and bring proper credit to myself and my family.

I now approach this day's demands with a proper calmness of heart, a truly clear mind and the ability to bring into appropriate action, my reserves of knowledge and ability. And having done my best Lord, to be satisfied with that. And if the results of this test are favourable, may I give you the glory.

Through Jesus Christ, my Lord, Amen.

(46) On accepting office

I bring to you in prayer, O God, the decision I have made to accept an office in the service of your church. I have done this after much thought, considerable reflection and also "taking it to the Lord, in prayer". It may be that I have some gift to offer. It must be my duty not to hold back that gift if it can be used in your service, Lord. "Take my gift and let it be consecrated, Lord, to thee".

I thank you, Lord, for the community that is your church, the fellowship in which the Holy Spirit moves, the "people of God" committed to your cause. It is a community in which there are diversities of gifts but "the same Lord" is the originator of them all. So there will be some with gifts of speaking, some of singing, some of teaching, some of leading worship, some with business experience who can help with finance and property, some with simple but important gifts, such as the gift of friendship (a gift not given to all equally), a sense of humour (very necessary even in holy circles), the ability to "make a good cup of tea". Let no one despise that last gift, Lord.

I approach this new undertaking in a spirit of humility, Lord. It is good that others have seen a talent in me which can be used in your cause. Enable me then to give freely of my abilities, always acting with sensitivity and consideration, never seeking to use my work for your church as a gateway to self-glorification, always contributing what I can give with generosity and joy.

So may the opportunity I have been given not only bless others, Lord. May it be a blessing to me.

In Jesus' name, Amen.

(47) Before a public address

As I prepare to address a meeting tonight, I think of your servant Moses, Lord, who, when called to witness to you, protested that he was not a good speaker. I ponder over what I have to say, aware of my limitations. But it is always my conviction that, if I call on your help, O God, you will not fail to be with me. I therefore commit the evening into your hands.

"How beautiful upon the mountains are the feet of those who bring good tidings!" said the prophet Isaiah. It is indeed a privilege to "speak a word for Jesus" and it is, in that spirit, I go forth to fulfil my task. But let me never undertake such a responsibility lightly, Lord. I must therefore do all I can to feed my mind, to read and to study and to reflect on the great truths of the faith. May I never speak arrogantly, but always with humility. May I at no time seek self-glory, always remembering whose I am and whom I serve. May I always leave behind the impression that "I have been with Jesus".

So, Lord, I give this evening completely into your hands, and pray that the thoughts that I express, and the words through which I express them, truly represent the essence of the Gospel of the kingdom.

Through Jesus Christ, my Lord, Amen.

(48) In advancing years

"Remember now your Creator in the days of your youth" the Preacher Ecclesiastes tells me, Lord. I feel an even greater need to remember as the years roll by when I am now "advanced in years". I do not find this an easy time, O God. It is all too easy to look back and realise one's shortcomings and failings, the opportunities missed, the harm I may have done. And what does the future hold, Lord? Failing strength, diminishing faculties, less mobility, lack of energy?

Is there any real value, Lord, in such negative reminiscence? The past is the past and that I cannot change, Lord. But there is something worse than that, Lord. Such rumination denies one of the most important areas of my belief, Lord. If, as I say whenever I recite the Creed, "I believe in the forgiveness of sins" and mean it, I have no right to dwell on my sins as if they were not forgiven. Your Word tells me that I am forgiven, Lord, and so, while I cannot undo the sins of the past, forgiven by you in Jesus, they have no longer power to damage me. This is the glorious truth of the Gospel, Lord.

So let me, in my advancing years, work and pray to nurture a true serenity, to create an inner peace soundly based on your unfailing love, your forgiveness, full and free. Let me realise that, though the physical body falters, my mind can be as active as ever. I have moreover the fruits of experience to offer and I can be of use to others.

May these years be, not a burden but a privilege, a time of hope, a time of achievement.

I ask all this in Jesus' name, Amen.

(49) On deciding to seek counselling

I have made a decision, Lord. I need help. I am not coping well with emotional tensions that are adversely affecting my life. I always thought I was strong enough to deal with any problems that might arise for me, Lord, but the truth is that I need to get support, to see everything more clearly and perhaps to look into my life and see if there are unresolved tensions arising out of my past experience that I need to understand.

It is not easy, Lord, to admit this need. I have coped successfully with difficult situations in both my personal and my professional life. And being as I am, a firm believer in prayer, I have been enabled, through confession, absolution and intercession, to see my way through difficult decisions and personal conflicts. But the strains and stresses of my life at this moment are in danger of overwhelming me completely. I believe that this admission of my need is the first step towards my reaching maturity and wholeness of being.

I know, Lord, that the counselling process will give me a safe and secure context in which to work towards a less tension-filled life. I am aware that, recently, I have not been easy to live with, and similarly, difficult to work with. I have brought strain into our home, leaving those with whom I have to do, puzzled and apprehensive. I acknowledge that I need help and for that help I will make application, Lord.

Without you, Lord, I can do nothing, so accompany me on this personal quest for self-knowledge and wholeness, and bring me a better quality of life that will be, not only a blessing to me, but also a real blessing to those with whom I have to do at work and play. May God truly be in my self-understanding.

I ask all this in Jesus' name, Amen.

(50) When called to jury service

"Judge not, that you be not judged", Jesus said. O God, I find that I am aware of these words as I open my mail this morning, for I have been asked to judge someone. Before me is a letter calling me up for service on a jury, and I tremble as I take it in. Am I suited to this task, Lord?

I am, of course, not really judging him or her, alleged to have committed a crime, but rather the evidence relating to their possible involvement in wrong-doing. The responsibility still feels awesome, Lord, especially if the crime is something very serious, such as murder. I may have to play a part in consigning someone to prison for life. But I cannot shrink from this duty. Grant me a clear head, O Lord, and sound judgement in my carrying out of this task.

It is all too easy, Lord, for sentiment to get in the way of rational decision. There is, unhappily, truth in the saying "There but for the grace of God, go I". This does not mean that, in hard fact, I too might commit an act of murder, although in desperate circumstances who knows what is possible? It is, however, saying what Jesus said to those who made accusations against the woman "taken in adultery": "let him who is not guilty of sin cast the first stone". We are, indeed, all imperfect beings. But our judicial system is based on trial by jury, and I must simply do my best to judge the evidence rightly and deliver an appropriate judgement.

This will be a humbling experience for me, Lord, but a salutary one. I will be under compulsion to be wholly objective in my assessment of all the circumstances involved, unprejudiced in my attitude, unmoved by any pressures such as the strong opinions of others. I must judge as I would be judged, Lord. So help me, God.

In Jesus' name, Amen.

(51) When gardening

How splendid is your creation, O God! The heavens declare your glory and the earth your handiwork. Here as I spend these holiday hours working in the garden, I feel the impact of this glorious truth and I rejoice that in what I am doing… digging, planting… I am sharing in the act of creation, Lord.

As I work, I pray, giving thanks for so much around me that is positive and good. I sense the order in the way your world works that speaks of a creator, Lord. The seasons come and go in sequence, the spring flowers always appear on time, the trees come alive again in their renewed green garments, the earth rests and revives each year. How impressive and reassuring I find this sense of providential but organised care. And what beauty there can be in a garden, Lord! My garden is a sea of colour. There is what seems to be an infinite variety of blooms around me and, as creation continues, new flowers will come, in their season, underlining the permanence of change in your creative work. For it all, I utter a deep-felt "Hallelujah!"

What a relief it is to be far from the tawdriness of so much daily life. Our world (and it is your world, O God) is, as I have said in prayer before, "a good thing spoiled". Material gain so dominates the life of the world today, multiplying greed. Greed breeds ruthlessness and a "me-first" philosophy far from the mind and teaching of Jesus. It is a blessed relief, O God, to be here and be reminded of another and a better world and for that blessing, I give you thanks, Lord.

In Jesus' name, Amen.

(52) When facing big decisions

At the centre of life, O God, there is decision-making and taking. It may be about my career. It may be about the person with whom I seek to spend my life. It may be about the children's education. In every aspect of my life, there are decisions to be made. Grant me, Lord, the will and, if necessary, the courage to calculate risks, see beyond the superficially attractive choice, and nail my colours to some worthwhile mast. And through whatever choices I make, Lord, may your will be done.

Decision-making demands a clear head, Lord, as well as a strong heart. That my education nourished my mind and, being at a school strong on sport, developed my body, I have no doubt. What is more difficult to create, Lord, is the maturity of personality essential for success in a demanding world. The need to make decisions is always there, Lord. But the choices change, becoming more complicated, creating more tension. Education must therefore go on and on, schooling us in coping in the university of life. I feel, however, the need of that additional quality, faith. I believe that you have a purpose for me, Lord, and so all my decisions must be made against the backdrop of your providential care. Only thus can I begin to trace your will and sense the vocation to which you may be calling me, Lord.

"Multitudes in the valley of decision" We are all there, Lord. Help us to choose wisely and well.

Through Jesus Christ, my Lord, Amen.

(53) After an evening at the theatre

For actors and actresses, playwrights and producers, directors and technicians, I give you thanks, this night, O God, for all have combined to create my evening at the theatre, an experience which, as well as entertaining me, has done me a great deal of good. This was a leisure time which I felt, in all honesty, that I deserved, but it was also one of learning for which I am grateful.

As in the realm of music, you give creative gifts to men and women, Lord, and so for centuries, there have been those who, taking the quill or the laptop, have drafted great scripts and stories and so produced great plays. What can we do but give thanks and praise for the genius of a Shakespeare in his time, or an Alan Bennett in ours?

The stage, like the cinema and the book, can be prostituted for unworthy and, often, evil purposes, Lord, and our world illustrates only too vividly, the curse of pornography and the false glorification of violence. Great industries thrive on the wrongful exploitation of the young and not so young. Unscrupulous vendors of vice care nothing so long as they make commercial gain. Chat line and online contacts open up dangerous opportunities for the innocent and the ignorant. I pray for a movement of the Spirit in our time, O God, a rushing mighty wind storming through the spiritual murkiness of today; a cleansing fire, purifying our common life, our entertainment, our media.

I thank you, O God, that what I have seen on stage tonight has been good and lovely and of very good report.

Through Jesus Christ, my Lord, Amen.

(54) On reading the daily newspaper

O God, how careless human beings can be; and how cruel! As I turn the pages of my newspaper, I tremble at the carelessness which causes accidents and hurt: I shudder at the cruelties of which human beings are capable. I feel the pain of the victims of both carelessness and cruelty, Lord. And in this I trust that I am "having the same attitude to life that Jesus had", and especially to its suffering. You wept, Lord Jesus, on hearing of the death of Lazarus, your friend. You cried as you contemplated Jerusalem and its bleak future. To see such compassion compels me to feel compassion too. As I read of earthquake, flood and fire, my heart bleeds for the utterly destitute and the sorely bereaved. As I am taken by reporters to battlefields and bomb-strewn roadsides, I tremble at the suffering so many, soldiers and civilians, women and children, as much as men, must undergo.

But so much worse, Lord, is the sheer cruelty of our times, of which my "daily" is so full. How awful is the cult of the knife and the dagger that has brought death to many in our time. How dreadful is the abuse inflicted on the innocent, sometimes by those claiming to be holy. How appalling are the crimes of murder and of rape that have ended innocent lives.

The reading of my newspaper is a summons to intercession, Lord. I must "pray without ceasing". That, Lord, may be all that I can do. But do it, I must.

Through Jesus Christ, my Lord, Amen.

(55) On writing a letter of condolence

How difficult is this task, O God. How hard it is to find words that adequately match my feelings. I have known this dear friend for so long that I feel her passing greatly. To have to write about her to her life's partner is indeed a heavy responsibility. But write I must, Lord, for his pain is greater than mine.

"Take with you words" God said to the prophet, Hosea. This is what I have to do, Lord, find words to express what I feel and to try to connect with what he is feeling. It is a daunting task, O God, but I must not shrink from it.

There is much power in a letter, Lord. How fully I understood this when I was bereaved and friends without number wrote to express sympathy and concern. Some found it hard to express their feelings and in trying to do that wrote at unnecessary length. Some tried hard to put their feelings into words and ended up unintentionally brusque. Some struggled to avoid sentimentality. Others wrote with conviction about their Christian hope and faith. All, Lord, tried to offer help, and did. Letters from friends can be a great blessing at such times. I received them gladly and criticise none.

As I prepare myself for this task, Lord, I do so with some temerity. I try to concentrate on my friend's needs at this time and not my own. It is not up to me to produce a work of art, a literary masterpiece or a definitive example of what a letter of condolence should be. What I have to do, Lord, is empathise with my friend's sadness and try to minister to that. My words must be simple but sincere. My concern must be for him and not for me.

I pray, Lord, that my letter of condolence will be a blessing to the one she left behind and in that spirit, I let it go, Lord.

In Jesus' name, Amen.

(56) When family members emigrate

My heart is sore today, O God. I have a sense of severe bereavement, two of my family having emigrated to Australia. It feels such a long way away, Lord, and it is not a mere holiday absence. This is for good, Lord, and I am bereft.

I understand why my family decided to take this step, Lord. Despite having degrees and qualifications, they just could not find jobs here. Frustrated beyond measure, they made their decisions, well aware of what it would all mean for me, to seek a fresh start in what they believe is a land of opportunity. I could not quarrel with those decisions, Lord. But it breaks my heart to see them go.

I know that nowadays Australia is just a plane journey away (at a cost) and that, all being well, I will see them again soon, that I must settle down to normal life. Help me to think of their needs, rather than mine, and to see what they have done not as a bereavement crisis but as a glorious opportunity.

Learning to live with separation is part of life, Lord. It is, however, not something to which I aspire easily and so, for some time, probably even for a long time, the pain of this separation will be very present with me. I therefore pray for the grace to cope with the hurt I feel, for I know my hurt is a burden on them at a time when they need to be focussed on their futures.

O God, I commit my loved ones to your safe keeping and pray for their well-being and prosperity.

In Jesus' name, Amen.

(57) On retiring

I come to this day, Lord, not with relief but with sadness. Young in heart, I am not ready to give up working, especially in a field that I love. But the calendar does not lie, Lord, and the time to retire has come.

"To work is to pray" it has been said, Lord. I have certainly found my work to have been a vocation and, in doing it, I have been greatly blessed. I hope too that what I have tried to do has blessed others on the way. I have over the years learned many things, Lord, the value of mutual dependence, the benefits of teamwork and cooperation, the importance of planning and the satisfaction of successful achievement. As I leave my office may I take away with me these gains and rewards, Lord.

Let me not treat this final day, Lord, as the end of everything, but rather as a new beginning, for there will now be time and opportunities that I have not had while working. There will be time to spend in the garden. There should be time for books and reading, in other words, time to do all the things for which there has been no time in a busy, working life. And there will be time for the family, for the grand-children, for friends, as well as time to serve you more fully through my church.

In the rearrangement of my life, O God, help me to ensure that there is time to wait upon you, Lord, to renew my strength, to develop my faith and to forward your kingdom.

I ask this prayer through Jesus Christ, my Lord, Amen.

(58) Approaching a General Election

It is your will that we should be good citizens, Lord, and this, as we approach a General Election, I seek so to be. It is my responsibility to respect authority, for so your Word teaches me, but only when that authority does justly and honours the way of uprightness and truth. In making my decision on how to vote in this Election, help me to keep in mind the need to honour the ten commandments and to consider the relative ability of the political parties involved to promote high standards of behaviour on the part, not only of members of parliament, but in every public sphere, business, social justice, law and order, and public ethics. May my vote not be partisan but principled. May I be motivated not by what I can get out of life for myself, but by the common good. May the member I choose to try to send to parliament be a man or woman of character and stature, seeking not personal gain but public improvement.

How overwhelming, O God, are the issues in politics today, the issues those I help to elect must face, the matters of war and peace, of the stewardship of national resources, of crime and punishment, of economics and economies. May those elected to serve in parliament bring humility and insight into every debate, faithfulness in attending to the interests of their constituents, irrespective of their political attachment, a willingness to listen rather than to declaim, respect for the integrity of political opponents. And may their guiding lights be not self-glorification, but service, for it is to that noble end, we are all called as good citizens and as disciples.

Through Jesus Christ, our Lord, Amen.

(59) After a visit to the library

How wonderful, O God, is the world of books! To spend an hour in the reference library is for me one of life's lovely activities. What numbers! What variety! Whatever developments there are in information technology, surely books will continue forever. I cannot conceive a world without books, Lord.

The time spent in my study, Lord, is an important part of my life. I see the making of books as a sphere through which I can honour you and serve you. As I continue to make this an essential part of my ministry, I ask for the presence of your enabling Spirit, Lord, for I truly believe that without your presence and guidance, I cannot meet the demands of authorship or the needs of those to whom I seek to minister through my books.

My frequent trips to the library arise from my need for both inspiration and information, Lord. That need for inspiration is crucial to my serving people, for every article that I write and every book I produce needs a theme and purpose. The library provides that inspiration. It leads me to new ideas, new perceptions, new arguments, the whole plethora of incoming information that widens my vision and develops my intelligence.

At the very centre of my life there is that one special book without which I could not live, the book I call the Word of God. In it there is myth and mystery, devotion and history, poetry and prophecy, letters and literature and, at its heart, there is the Gospel story presenting Jesus, not as fiction, but as fact, telling the story of the birthday of the church through the coming of the Spirit and the witness of your servants, laying out the promises and privileges of Christian discipleship, pointing at all times to Jesus, the crucified and risen Lord. How glorious is this book of books, Lord!

The love of books is no passing phase, Lord. Books will accompany me through every stage of my life. Grant me then the opportunity often to pay a visit to the library.

In Jesus' name, Amen.

(60) When frustrated by technology

O God, I give you thanks for the miracles of modern information technology, for the computer, the printer and the endless facilities the computer makes available. That such gifts of exploration and invention have been given to mankind is one of the wonders of your creation, O God. May such gifts be used for the enhancement of modern living and the extension of knowledge in the whole community.

I see the benefits of such developments in the small context of my life, Lord. I can produce a much better quality than I used to be able to do, in correspondence and manuscripts. I can communicate by e-mail, with amazing speed, Lord, right across the world. I can tap into a vast amount of information and knowledge through the internet making immediate research possible. For such benefits I am truly grateful, O God.

As with gifts of creation, Lord, there is the possibility of abuse as well as use. And abuse a-plenty there will be, Lord. There are those who will use these new facilities for pornographic pleasure, as a means to abuse children, as a mechanism for encounters that can end up in crime, Lord. I pray you, O God, in your loving mercy, prevent and forestall all who have evil intensions from exploiting these new fields.

Grant me patience, Lord, in the use of these facilities. All forms of technology, including everything mechanical, can develop faults. Help me to understand that these things are not "sent to try us" by some malevolent agency but are simply the difficulties inherent in inventions conceived by human minds and created by human hands.

This prayer I bring, in Jesus' name, Amen.

(61) Before writing a book

I face my greatest challenge yet, Lord. I have been asked to write a book. The prospect fills me with anxiety, because of the scope of the project. How can I produce one hundred thousand words on any subject, Lord? For this is what I have to do. And within a specified time, Lord. My spirit wilts at the thought of such a project. But can I turn down such a challenge, Lord?

From my earliest years, I have sought to be a writer, Lord. Even as a child I was drawn to words on paper. And through the years, the desire to write has never left me, Lord. I turned to freelance journalism as a hobby, but this is something far more demanding, Lord. Dare I turn down the opportunity?

What I have been asked to do is write a popular biography of a public figure in the religious field. I have never met this person or even heard of her, but in her own country she is, as they say these days, Lord, a "legend". I shall have to go and meet her, Lord, and if I find her story appeals to me and is likely to appeal to others, I must then decide if this is something I should do.

I come to you now, Lord, six months further on. I have met and interviewed the subject of my proposed book, and have been inspired by her story and achievements. I have no doubt that it is your will that I should carry out this task as a service to you and to your cause. I therefore commend this, my first attempt at a book, to your care, Lord, and pray that my work too will be to your glory.

Through Jesus Christ, my Lord, Amen.

(62) Before going to the dentist

I have dreaded the coming of this day, Lord. And how foolish I feel about it! For so long, I have hated going to the dentist. It is not that he is an unpleasant man. He is friendly and considerate, as well as understanding of my fears and phobias. But I dislike the process so much… the very thought of the drilling or the extracting makes me tense and strained, Lord. Is it childhood memories of similar unpleasant interventions? Or later experiences that were painful in the extreme? I do not know, Lord, but I am aware that, from the dawning of this day, my nerves have been taut, Lord, and I dread the approach of the appointed hour.

We human beings are vulnerable to physical ailments that make dentists, doctors, nurses, midwives, surgeons, and so many other people, important to us, and I give you thanks that there are those who spend years of training in order to look after us. I give you thanks, Lord, that so many are not only skilled but also compassionate, bearing patiently with our anxieties and fears.

Of my gratitude for all such help, including that of my dentist, Lord, there is no doubt, but, as I set off towards the surgery, I still struggle to contain my fear. To be neither troubled nor afraid in these circumstances, Lord, is just beyond my frail human ability, but summoning up my sense of responsibility, I try, in all sincerity, to put myself in your hands… and his, and know that in but a short time, I shall be on my way home again, relaxed and relieved.

Amen! So let it be, Lord!

(63) On a visit to the Holy Land

What a thrill it was, O God, to fly in over the Mediterranean Sea and look down on, for the first time, the land where Jesus lived his short life, but on which he left a huge and lasting impression. How eagerly I look forward to see all this close at hand. What is, at this stage, most moving is the sense of reality and authenticity, this experience is bringing to me.

How important, Lord, is this journey of a lifetime! For so long I have read about your life on earth. Now, in the hot and dusty streets inside the walls of Jerusalem, I somehow sense the presence of the living, Lord. And this feeling becomes the more intense as I trudge up the narrow cobbled way, the Via Dolorosa, and think of our Lord, surrounded by hostile crowds, followed by Simon of Cyrene carrying the cross, making his way towards his ultimate Calvary. No wonder, Lord, there was thick darkness during the hour of his crucifixion! No wonder an earthquake rocked Jerusalem! Was nature itself protesting against the unwarranted suffering of your Son?

Already I feel the impact of walking "in the steps of the Master", Lord. The sheer cruelty of the treatment meted out to Jesus beggars belief. The absolute injustice perpetrated on one who, innocent, was led, like a lamb, to its slaughter cries "Shame!" But once again, Lord, I realise this is not fiction but history. Did ever human beings conceive such a crime?

I am deeply moved, Lord, as I tread the roads that Jesus trod and feel, in a new way, the story of his crucifixion. "Lord, is it !?" The only possible response to this searching question is abject confession and profound repentance.

Through Jesus Christ, my Lord, Amen.

(64) By the Sea of Galilee

Lord, as I stand here on a hill above Tiberias, I look down, with profound emotion, on the Sea of Galilee. What images it conjures up, Lord! Where Jesus walked on the water! Where he stilled the storm! Where he preached to the throngs on the shore from a boat! How strange it is to think that what I am seeing, he saw too. And when, later, I shall sail across to the other side of the water, I shall be replicating his journey. How real it all makes the incarnation, Lord!

Such a moment as this calls up the wonder of Jesus' life, the marvellous miracles he did, the teaching he proclaimed and everything that formed his life on earth. His goodness was so great that I can never approach that level but he has, at least, given me an example and an aim. If, through your grace, I can inch my way towards a greater goal, I will be blessed indeed.

How good it is, Lord, to follow in Jesus' footsteps and underline memories of his love and grace. To be in Cana made his first miracle (according to your servant, John), real. To see Nazareth, where he was brought up, made real his humanity: he was, as we are, part of a family, a community, a nation. He worked at a trade as ordinary people do. By going missing to talk to scholars and wise men, he caused his parents anxiety as we can do. These human things so strongly underline his real humanity, Lord. To know he was truly human is a great blessing to us, Lord.

How blessed I am, Lord, to be walking in the steps of the Master! To be seeing the sights he saw, to be sailing on the water on which he walked, how gloriously real it makes your Word! How very, very moving it makes our experience.

O God, I am glad to be here! To walk and climb and sail "in my Master's steps" is inspiration, indeed.

In Jesus' name, Amen.

Section 4

Times and Seasons: 65-85

(65) At the changing of the clocks as Spring approaches

How I welcome this day, O God! The clocks "spring forward" to help us realise that the days of winter darkness are ending. What a blessing the approach of spring is! Signs of new life are all around us. The snowdrops bloom. The crocuses light up the borders. The gay daffodils and narcissi decorate the parks. The trees begin to bud and soon the May blossom will appear. What a wonderful gift is Nature's resurrection, a glad certainty that we can anticipate with total confidence. O God, that you are indeed at work in the world, constantly creating, constantly re-creating.

You "make all things new". You are our shepherd and we shall never want. You take us to and through green pastures, acknowledging our need of sustenance. You lead us by the still waters to restore our souls. And when, in the turbulence of life, we have to pass through the shadows, you promise your continual presence with us. Truly, goodness and mercy do accompany us all the days of our lives. And the resurrection of life that we see, Lord, in the cycles of nature, point us to the ever present reality of the gift of new life in the Spirit.

You are, O God, light ever-breaking through the darkness of this world to bring illumination, clarity and understanding to us all. So thank you for the symbolism of the changing of the clocks, enabling us to have more light.

Lighten our darkness, O Lord, I pray.

In Jesus' name, Amen.

(66) When Spring has come

What a joyous time, spring is, Lord! To see everywhere the signs of new life brings uplift and inspiration. Gone at last, Lord, are those dark and dreary winter days that pulled me down and made me long for the coming of spring. Now all around me are the green shoots that tell me that my garden will soon show growth, that send me back to my allotment to dig and plant, that confirm for me again the constancy of the divine providence, that assures me that you are still the Creator, ever faithful, ever sure.

How thrilling it is to believe and to know, too, that you, our God, who is the Creator, is still active in creation. What glorious good news! And so the Holy Spirit, sent by you to be our Comforter, like the wind, blows through your world to assure us of the divine creativity, inspiring those sensitive to his presence to produce works of wonder and beauty for our inspiration and encouragement.

Continue, O God, your creative work. Raise up gifted men and women who can compose and write, artists who can draw and paint, sculptors who can fashion statues out of stone, actors who can bring to life the playwright's themes, conductors who can turn numerous players into a harmonious whole. Give profundity of knowledge to philosophers and theologians, so that we may understand more of the meaning of life. Produce good men and women in every walk of life, people of integrity in the professions, men and women of skill in the trades, and those who are physically strong to fulfil labouring tasks, innovators, inventors and scientists exploring the as yet unknown reaches of the universe.

So for the joys of spring, O God, I give you thanks.

Through Jesus Christ, our Lord, Amen.

(67) "Summer suns are glowing…"

What a joy it is, O God, when, as the old hymn says "Summer suns are glowing". How great is the beauty of the earth when the sun shines brightly on it! How pleasant is summer warmth with long evenings extending the joy of being in the open air! There is much to give thanks for, O Lord, in this splendid season of the year.

As I contemplate the summer sunshine, Lord, I reflect on the seasons, the stages of our lives. When the springtime of youthfulness has gone, there comes the summertime in our lives, the middle years that should be characterised by maturity and productivity. It is a time when energy is in good supply, when thoughts are positive, and when the mind is at its best. These are the years when we are as able as we shall ever be to take things in our stride, Lord, to be properly creative, to have an influence on the world around us.

At the same time, Lord, storms can break on us in summer days… the unexpected crisis, a financial disaster, a health breakdown. But this, Lord, is the story of life itself. It is a time in which we have to summon up all the certainties of our faith. Give us the grace to face whatever life brings to us with a calm serenity and a proper hope. Our extremity is your opportunity, Lord. If we remain faithful, you will bring us, through our experiences, unexpected blessings.

Enable us, O God, to enjoy our summer-time in both the seasonal and the spiritual sense.

In Jesus' name, Amen.

(68) In the Autumn

With the approach of autumn, comes mixed feelings for me, O Lord. It is the season of glorious colours, creating golden splendour across my garden. But it is too a time when so much in nature dies and the leaves begin to fall. Perhaps, O God, this speaks to me of where I am in life; in one way in the golden years but in another, days of decline.

Let me, Lord, use these autumn days to assess my life afresh. While there are so many ways in which I have failed and failed badly.. and this I freely acknowledge, Lord, with a penitent heart, there are successes too. I have worked hard in the service of men and women. I have followed my vocation although it could never make me rich. I have spent long hours on heavy tasks, maybe to the detriment of my own welfare and health. I feel it is right, Lord, that I should recognise such achievements as now I assess, equally, my failures. And of these I have no doubt, Lord. For such failures, I ask your forgiveness.

As I go through these changing autumn days, Lord, may I use them to reassess my purposes, my aims. Help me especially to use the accumulated experience of my spring and summer years to determine how the autumn should be spent. I know now that I should wait on the Lord in every project, rather than just rushing at it, unprepared and immature. I know now that, if what I am doing is in accordance with your will, that project will be blessed. I know that walking in humility is of the essence of the faith too.

For the benefits and blessings of experience, I give you thanks, Lord. If I would live, I must learn.

In Jesus' name, Amen.

(69) At the changing of the clock as Winter approaches

"Spring forward, fall back" they say, O God. Alas, this is, again, fallback time and, as autumn slips away, winter approaches. The light nights of summer, when we could do so much, are long gone and the changing of the clock underlines the hard fact that the darkness of the winter nights has returned.

I do not like the darkness, O God. It speaks to me of unpleasant things. I recall that Judas Iscariot, set on betraying Jesus, went out from the company of the disciples to carry out his foul deed, and Scripture records that, when he did so, it was night. How symbolic that feels, Lord. Night is the time of the burglar and others intent on crime. And symbolically again, at the precise time of Jesus' death on the cross, there was darkness over all the land.

It is not, however, for my good that I meet this change of time so negatively, Lord. I do not need to feel depressed (as I could so easily) by such a circumstance. Let me rather turn this day into a "window of opportunity". There is so much that I can do in the comfort of my home, the books that I can read, the correspondence on which I can catch up, perhaps even the articles I could research and write. There is time too, to engage in some serious study. And more than that, there is the opportunity to be with family, to invite some friends. For these positive aspects of unwelcome darkness, I give you thanks, O God.

Through this particular event, may I re-learn the need to be positive at all times, to accept and redeem unwelcome circumstances and to ensure that I get the best out of life, come darkness or, in due time, come light.

In Jesus' name, Amen.

(70) In the bleak mid-winter

How bleak and cold is the winter time, O God. How difficult it is to keep warm and well. The days are short. The dark nights are long. And as the years go by, Lord, my ability to cope with ice and snow, rainstorms and strong winds decreases, Lord, as does my resistance to viruses and germs. But, O my God, let me not wallow in self-pity. My lot is cast in pleasant places, free from the extremes that bring death and destruction to faraway places. My blessings are there to be counted, Lord. And they are many. Thanks be to you, O God.

I come to you, O God, in intercession for the thousands of victims of nature's disasters, where flood and earthquake, wind and fire bring death to whole communities, with homes wrecked, businesses destroyed, families wiped out. O hear me, Lord, too when I cry to you for those in peril on the sea.

I thank you, O God, for all those who, by their attention to health and safety, ensure our safe passage through life, those who supply our warmth, deliver our food, provide our clothes, attend to our needs. And may I not only receive these blessings but do all I can to ensure that no one, in their need, is left unnoticed and uncared for. In the dark winter days, may I find joy in the knowledge that spring will surely come as dawn follows dusk and day succeeds night. So may I, strong in my faith and buoyed up by my hope, go forward, trusting in the divine consistency that never fails.

Through Jesus Christ, my Lord, Amen.

(71) In the season of Advent

"Hark, the glad sound, the Saviour comes!" "O come, O come, Immanuel!" It is the season of Advent, and I rejoice in it, indeed. It is, for me, a time of joy, a season of peace, a ground of hope. At the very centre of my faith is the one who will come as the little child of Bethlehem, welcomed by singing angels, dumbstruck shepherds, and respectful wise men, but the one who will be "crucified under Pontius Pilate", "despised and rejected of men, a man of sorrows and acquainted with grief". "He died that we might be forgiven". He rose again that we might receive the gift of "eternal life". Welcome, Lord Jesus!

Advent is, for me, that "ground of hope". "I may not know, I cannot tell, what shame he had to hear but I believe it was for me, he hung and suffered there". Advent tells me that I do not have to earn salvation: it is the Lord's gift. As one liable to the sins of the flesh, I will never be able to manifest goodness, purity and holiness but Advent tells me that, through this man, the Christ, there will come "the fruits of the Spirit". Come then O long-expected Jesus! Bring us your Advent gifts of grace!

This is a time for recollection and reflection, for memory and meditation. "Those who walked in darkness", myself included, have seen a great light, for "Unto us a child is born, unto us a son is given, and his name shall be called wonderful Counsellor, mighty God, everlasting Father, Prince of Peace".

As this season of Advent begins, to that I say "Amen".

Through Jesus Christ, my Lord, Amen.

(72) As the season of Lent begins

Lent is, for me, Lord, a time of spiritual pilgrimage and therefore of renewal. To spend these days in the company of Jesus is of enormous value to me, Lord. From the moment when he "set his face" to go to Jerusalem, completely and totally aware of all that was going to happen to him until Easter morning brought the final moment of triumph, he was determined to fulfil your will, whatever pain it brought. I find joining (as far as I can) in that journey brings me greater understanding of the cost of his journey.

The next line of that hymn, Lord, is "and we must love him too", so Lent is, for me, Lord, a time of re-dedication and commitment, a time of "trying his work to do". I therefore dedicate this Lenten season to sustained discipleship and making every effort to grow into the likeness of Jesus by using the means of grace, provided for us.

How conscious I am of how far short of the standards of the Kingdom I fall. How, usually unintentionally, I "crucify Jesus afresh and put him to open shame". With each of the disciples, I want to say, when you have been let down, "Is it I, Lord?" But let me not wallow in self-condemnation, Lord, or seek to drown myself in self-pity. We are not in despair. Because of the ultimately triumphant Christ, we are people with hope, with purpose, with intent, with faith.

I come to this Lent with humility but with hope, Lord. I pray that it may be, for me, truly a time of "grace, mercy and peace".

Through Jesus Christ, my Lord, Amen.

(73) On Mothering Sunday

On this day of thanksgiving for mothers everywhere, I give you thanks, O God, for Mary, the mother of our Lord. She was indeed "blessed among women". And she had the character to match her calling, Lord, being sensitive to her son's vocation, prayerfully "pondering in her heart" whatever she saw him do, whatever she heard him say. Ever present with him in his life and death, she would join in fellowship and prayer with the disciples after his resurrection, she, too, a faithful servant to you, O God, and one in whom you could delight.

I give you thanks, O God, for the gifts that women, and not least mothers, bring to discipleship… tenderness, sensitivity, thoughtfulness and that instinctive caring concern that leads to self-sacrifice for their children's needs. I pray that the gentle graces of femininity be brought to bear on human problems, leading to conciliation and reconciliation.

May mothers, Lord, do all they can to campaign against war, crusade for the welfare of every child whatever their background, colour or race, confront whoever harms one little one, condemn careless authorities, whose inefficiency leads to abuse and hurt, contribute to a better, kindlier world. Bind mothers together in the unity of the Spirit, creating a force for good that can overcome the world.

For every woman privileged to be a mother, for Mary, privileged to be the mother of Jesus, I give you thanks, O God, this Mothers' Day.

Through Jesus Christ, my Lord, Amen.

(74) On Maundy Thursday

He is the greatness, the power and the glory, O God, but what do I see that same Jesus doing on this Maundy Thursday but an action of loving humility? For there he is, washing his disciples' feet! That one who need not have counted it as "robbery" to claim equality with you should undertake such a lowly act is beyond my comprehension. But it happened, Lord. It is authentic, it is true. Such humility impels me to reverential praise.

To demonstrate genuine humility is so difficult for people like me, O God, for was it not blatant pride, the belief that men and women could be like God, that led to punishment in the Garden of Eden? How prone we human beings are to "lean on our own understanding", to say "But who is God that we need be mindful of him?" Forgive us, Lord.

I come to you today, O God, to ask you to help me to "walk humbly with you, my God". As I look to Jesus and see in him life as it should be; as I watch him during his ministry on earth and see his ever-present graciousness; as I journey with him through Lent and come to understand his capacity for obedience, the more I realise how far I am from the kingdom, Lord.

I pray that you will turn this Maundy Thursday into a day of dedication, Lord. So may this day be for me a day of spiritual growth, a day of grace at the end of which I can truly say "Nearer I am, O God, to thee. Nearer to thee".

Through Jesus Christ, my Lord, Amen.

(75) On Good Friday

"We may not know", Lord. "We cannot tell", Lord, "what pains Jesus had to bear. But we believe", Lord that "it was for us he hung and suffered there". How true this is, Lord. As with humble reverence and silent worship, I come into your presence, O God, on this holy day, I am struck dumb at the cost of what our Lord endured for me and all mankind.

As I reflect on the events of that day, which culminated in crucifixion, how awful, O God, was the behaviour among Jesus' contemporaries. Hypocritical religious authorities, totally blind to, not only mercy, but basic justice! A Roman governor washing his hands of responsibility and offering a criminal, Barabbas, in Jesus' place! A totally insensitive mob of people crying "Crucify him! Crucify him!" And his disciples? "They all forsook him and fled". Is this not totally unbelievable, Lord? Yet these are the facts, this is history. The "man of sorrows" was "despised and rejected of men", was nailed to a cross, nature demonstrating its sense of cosmic disturbance with earthquakes and "gross darkness" over all the land.

And so, with a humble heart and deep penitence, I affirm as surely multitudes will confirm: "Surely he has borne our griefs and carried our sorrows". "There was no other good enough", Lord. "O dearly, dearly has he loved". Words fail me, Lord, before this the greatest of all the mysteries of suffering.

And so, O God, I spend this day, in silent adoration. No words of mine can truly reflect the sense of gratitude I feel, on this Good Friday. "Were the whole realm of nature mine, it were an offering far too small", Lord. "Love so amazing, so divine, demands my soul, my life, my all".

Through Jesus Christ, my Lord, Amen.

(76) On Holy Saturday

It is Holy Saturday, Lord God, and, as I am taught to believe, Jesus, on this day, "descended into hell". I am not sure that I understand this, Lord, but what I sense is that Jesus goes to the very lowest depths in an act of loving rescue. This, O Lord, is the glorious news on this holy Saturday. There is nowhere beyond the reach of your unfailing love. This is good news, indeed, Lord.

I see myself, in all honesty, Lord, as the worst of sinners. There are totally unacceptable things that I have done, which are an intolerable burden on my mind. At times, I sinned innocently. At other times, I sinned wilfully, aggressively pushing aside conscience, the still, small voice within me, to enjoy the wrong-doing on which I was intent. But there is yet more, Lord. It is that I am all too aware that there is within me a corruption common to all mankind, a condition to which your servant, Paul, confessed and which led him to cry out in spiritual agony: "Who shall deliver me from this death?" On this Holy Saturday, because Jesus descended into hell, I can say, with him: "I thank God, through Jesus Christ, my Lord". This is the good news. Thanks be to you, O God.

And so, O God, this Holy Saturday brings me comfort and assurance beyond belief. There is no depth to which I can fall that is beyond the redeeming embrace of your love. I therefore spend this holy Saturday "safe in the arms of Jesus". What grounds for "wonder, love and praise"!

Through Jesus Christ, my Lord, Amen.

(77) On Easter Day

"The Lord is risen, is risen indeed. Hallelujah!" Let the universal acclamation ring out across the world – Jesus lives!

What a glorious sense of freedom this Easter Day brings, O God. "Death has no more dominion over us" we read in the Good Book. "The strife is o'er, the battle won" we sing. How central to our faith is this joyous day, Lord. "If we do not believe that Christ has risen from the dead" your servant, Paul, says, "we are, of all people, the most unhappy". Let me then share, Lord, in the universal Christian affirmation that this, the most important day in the Christian year, brings: "The Lord is risen indeed!"

For Mary Magdalene, for the apostles, even for doubting Thomas, for the two disciples who found that their unknown companion on the way to Emmaus was indeed the risen Lord, there was an overwhelming sense of joy in the knowledge that Jesus was still with them. So is it for me, Lord, and for the Christian church. Jesus has fulfilled his promise that he would not "leave us desolate", but would be with us still, "even to the end of the world".

O God, serene in the knowledge that Jesus lives, sharing my joys, empathising with my sorrows, understanding my weakness, so my pilgrimage goes on, that "other Comforter", the Holy Spirit, sustaining me. "I do not ask to see the distant scene", Lord, "one step enough for me". But in that step, I know, this Easter Day, that you are with me. The Lord is risen, is risen indeed!

In Jesus' name, I ask this prayer, Amen.

(78) On Ascension Day

What a day for the disciples, Lord! To see Jesus ascend to heaven before their very eyes made it natural for them "to stand gazing upwards", transfixed. This is one miracle more for them to try to understand… Transfiguration, Crucifixion, The Descent into Hell, the Resurrection and now The Ascension. Then came angelic voices that brought them back to earth. "Why are you standing here, gazing up to heaven?" they ask. They are ready with an immediate reply, a call to action. This is not a time for silent contemplation. It is the time for action. Life shaping events are on the way. The Holy Spirit will shortly come with power from on high.

I want to, quite properly, spend part of this Ascension Day in silent wonderment and adoration, Lord, but I too have to hear the call to action and involvement. The Christian life is no static ceremony, Lord. It is a constant call to witness and service. So let me too be thrilled by Jesus' ascension to be "at the right hand of God", but always in order to be more ready to "serve you as you deserve", O God.

The ascension experience was a significant stage on a journey for a group of perplexed and uncertain men. For me, though the journey is different, the essential elements are the same, Lord. We are pilgrims, living in an active relationship with the risen and ascended Jesus. The gift of the Holy Spirit has been given to us. Wherever we must go and whatever we must do, you are, Immanuel, "God with us". That means we will always be given the words that we must speak. It means that, though in this world we may well have tribulation, Lord, you will be there too for you have "overcome the world".

I thank you, Lord, for both the excitement and the wonder of this Ascension Day. I see the Lord Jesus, "high and lifted up" in glory, but I see him too walking beside me on the road that leads to life. What a glorious promise this Ascension day brings! What a wonderful degree of assurance it brings with it, Lord.

In Jesus' name, Amen.

(79) At Pentecost

I welcome this day, O God, for it is Whitsuntide, Pentecost, the birthday of the church. What a glorious day, a day to remember when mighty wind and flaming tongues announced the coming of your Holy Spirit. "You shall have power" Jesus had told the disciples. What power, Lord! Fearful, ordinary men were filled with the Spirit and set out to conquer the world… in Jesus' name. And here am I, Lord, two thousand years on, continuing to try to repeat the first disciples' aim, striving to proclaim, in whatever way I can that Jesus is Lord, that you, God are "unfailing love", that the power of the Holy Spirit is with us today.

I love to hear the story of the Church of Jesus, Lord, for it is the evidence for the ongoing work of the Holy Spirit. Despite many failures and failings, you constantly raise up prophets and preachers, who will haul the church back on to "the Way". Always in need of reform, your church, thankfully, has sought to understand its failures and learn lessons. I thank you, Lord, especially, for the recognition of the need to return to your Word and make that the solid foundation for the church's belief and consequent action. For I know, Lord, that only on that basis can the church grow and expand.

Come, Holy Spirit, come… today, now. "Dispel the darkness from our minds", Lord, "and open all our eyes". Send the wind of your Spirit to blow through every part of the church's life, purifying it, transforming it, renewing it. Let the fire of the Spirit energise the church, Lord, and enthuse those who belong to it with fresh zeal. And may this whole process of positive change begin with me, Lord.

Through Jesus Christ, my Lord, Amen.

(80) At the season of All Saints

"For all the saints who from their labours rest", may your name be forever blessed, O God. So sings the church. And as I reflect on the meaning of this season of All Saints, so I give thanks for all those who have passed to their rest having added to my life by their gifts and love. I think of my parents and all they gave up that I might have a good life. I think of those true saints of yours, O God, whose commitment and zeal for your kingdom have influenced my own love for you. I think of those who died too young, taken away before they had enjoyed fullness of life. I think of those who had to endure great suffering in their later years, who have passed to that realm where there is no more pain.

What a blessing it is to be able to keep in mind forever, the moments that should never be forgotten, the great ceremonial times affecting me and my loved ones, the generosity and kindnesses given to me without thought of return, the encouragement I have received when struggling, the comfort that I have received when grieving, the thanks that I have received for things that I have done, the forgiveness vouchsafed to me, when I did not do what I ought to do.

May the influence of the memories in this season of All Saints be demonstrated in the future quality of my life, and may the consciousness of my being part of a great company stretching beyond the bounds of earth and reaching into heaven, provide a stimulus to my spiritual life that will produce the fruit of the Spirit one hundred-fold.

I ask this prayer in Jesus' name, Amen.

(81) On Remembrance Day

How awesome, Lord, is the silence, I, like all others, will observe on this Remembrance Day! That the nation should stand still for these moments is right and proper lest we forget the sacrifices of war. In thousands of homes there will be heavy-hearted memories of those who went to war and failed to return. In rehabilitation hospitals, those maimed for life will still be found, never to be able-bodied again. How awful is war, Lord! The sheer horror of the trenches in the First World War. The terror of flying bombs and rockets in the Second World War. Wars to end wars, Lord? But they go on (The Falklands) and on (Iraq) and on (Afghanistan). How long, Lord? How long?

The politics of power still rule the world. The nuclear threat remains. New ideologies create new threats. Space exploration becomes the prostitution of discovery for military advantage. And so conflict embraces not only the earth, Lord. It reaches the heavens.

O God, I pray that this Remembrance Day may focus not only on a gratitude that looks back in awe at sacrifices made. Rather turn our eyes and thoughts to international reconciliation and a universal determination to seek peace and pursue it. May the leaders of the nations unite to share the marvels and products of this wonderful world that you, in love, created, giving priority to those parts of the world which, underdeveloped as they are, teem with populations that they cannot feed.

O God, the roots of war are in the loveless hearts and selfish minds of human beings. The transformation of human nature remains the priority at the heart of the search for peace. Then let us all, with contrite hearts, unite in prayer for the power of the Spirit to bring about change. Amen, so let it be, Lord, on this Remembrance Day.

In Jesus' name, Amen.

(82) On Christmas Eve

O still and silent night! O holy night! The "hopes and fears of all the years are met in you tonight"… somehow. For, with all Christendom, I share the expectation for which this silent, holy night stands, the coming of you, O God, into the world. And what expectations we have! The redemption of our sins! The possibility of inner peace! The assurance that you are "God with us"! Let all your people join in glad exclamation, Lord! "Come, thou long-expected Jesus!"

What longing, what yearning runs through the whole Old Testament story as the people of God look for the coming of Messiah! The one who will deliver them and "restore Israel"! A mighty conqueror! A national hero! But what, this night, are we given? A little child, born not in noble surroundings, but lying in a manger somewhere in an inn in Bethlehem. Nor would he grow, Lord, into a warrior king. For his destiny would be, as one prophet foretold, that of the suffering servant.

It is in the fulfilment of that prophecy our salvation lies, Lord. He willingly took the form of a servant. He was found in fashion as a man. He became obedient unto death, even death on a cross. And, as he himself so boldly promised: in three days he would rise again.

O still and silent night! O holy night! What divine drama, Lord! Grant me a humble heart as I, with all who love you, look once more to celebrate this extraordinary, wonderful, deeply moving Christmas story.

In Jesus' name, Amen.

(83) On Christmas Day

This, O God, is a day that you have made! How can we not rejoice and be glad in it? The Word has, in the person of a little child, become flesh and he will live among us. And we shall behold his glory, full of grace and truth. O, happy day!

Bless me and all who, as Christians, bear the name of Jesus as, on this holy day, we journey once again through the magic events of the Christmas story. We hurry with the wondering shepherds from the hills above Bethlehem to find Jesus, lying in a manger. We travel with the wise men, our eyes on the guiding star, and see them offer their costly gifts… gold, frankincense and myrrh. We stay in thought with Joseph and Mary, your devoted servants, Lord: Joseph a man of dignity and honour, accepting what he could not understand, sensitive to your directing of him as to your will. Mary, devout, holy, chosen to be the mother of our Lord because she truly was your "handmaid". O God, I honour these two wonderful people.

For this family day of gladness and celebration, I give you thanks, O God. For the opportunity to be together, free from the daily distractions of ordinary life, I thank you. In all our fun, fellowship and the sharing of food, may I never lose sight of the reason for our celebration, namely that you so loved the world that you gave your Son so that all who believe in him will have "everlasting life".

This indeed, O God, is the day that you have made. For the hope and joy it brings, I give you my heartfelt thanks and praise.

Through Jesus Christ, my Lord, Amen.

(84) On New Year's Eve

"Count your blessings; name them one by one. And it will surprise you what the Lord has done". So runs an evangelical hymn, Lord, that I have known all my life. How true it feels now as the year that is passing slips slowly away. I have been greatly blessed, Lord. I recall many instances of your continual care, the times when, as I said at the time, Lord: "This is God's doing and is it not marvellous in our eyes?" The ways in which things have so often "worked together for good" have had a huge impact on me. The continual arrival of "divine surprises" has moved me deeply. But there are those other times too, Lord, when I have not only hoped for, but I have prayed for a particular blessing, and the answer I wanted just did not come. These are the times when my faith has been tested, tests survived because of my overwhelming belief in your providential care. For what I have learned of your will and your ways, O Lord, I offer praise and thanksgiving.

I willingly make confession of all my sins, Lord. I know that life is a constant struggle to resist temptation. When I have not yielded to such temptation, it is your saving grace at work within me. When I have failed and done "the evil that I would not" or failed to do "the good that I should", you have always been there, arms outstretched, in loving acceptance. I thank you, Lord, that I can end this year by confessing, heartily and enthusiastically, that "I believe in the forgiveness of sins".

So, Lord, I lay this year to rest and turn my eyes to tomorrow and the year to come. The past I entrust to your care, O God. For the future, bless me with abundant grace.

Through Jesus Christ, my Lord, Amen.

(85) On New Year's Day

"Teach me, good Lord, to serve you as you deserve, to give and not to count the cost, to fight and not to heed the wounds, to toil and not to seek for rest, to labour and to ask for no reward, save the knowledge that we do your will". On this, the first day of a new year, I re-dedicate myself to you in the words of your servant, Saint Francis. Hear my prayer, Lord.

I value this day, O God, because it brings me the chance to begin again. I therefore pray for the strength of will to make, honour and keep the resolutions and promises it is in my heart to prepare. There are the responsibilities I owe to my family, the need to give them time and love. There are the duties I owe as a citizen, to stand for the things "that are good and lovely, and of good report". There are obligations I have as a member of the human family, to campaign and crusade for justice for all, for the inherent value of every human being and for the obliteration of every kind of racial intolerance.

May I enter this day, O God, with profound hope, with strong faith and filled with love for you and all mankind. May that love instil in me a compassion that reaches out to anyone in need and that makes me generous when tragedy strikes. And may the attitudes I display and the behaviour I demonstrate be an indication to all that, as I have said in prayer at other times, "I have been with Jesus".

Lord, let this new year be dedicated to the extension of all that is right and good. So may it be one of countless blessings for me, for those I love and for all for whom I pray.

In Jesus' name, Amen.

Section 5

In the spiritual life: 86-100

(86) When spiritually drained

In all my working life, I have tried to do my best, Lord, to fulfil expectations, both those of myself and of others. I have been consistent in my application, enthusiastic in the pursuit of all I am asked to do, energetic in my efforts to accomplish my objectives. But tonight, Lord, I have reached something of a crisis. I need to look again at my life, and my work, in relation to my life. Let me then bring all this to you in prayer, O God, and see it all in the light of your purpose for me.

"Seek first the Kingdom of God and its righteousness" Jesus says "and other things will be added to you". I reflect on these words, Lord, and try to apply them to my motivation and application. As I think on these things, I feel that Jesus did not have in mind the *amount* of time to be allocated to this and to that. I suspect he was talking of *proportion*, about the way we look at life, Lord. And maybe that is where I am going wrong, Lord. Not intentionally, but in reality. I am letting the "other things", that is the worldly, material things I have to do, so consume me that I am spiritually drained. I need renewal, Lord.

Let me be still, O Lord, this night and approach tomorrow and the work I have to do, with a fresh outlook. And whatever I am doing, may I do it "as unto the Lord", with graciousness and grace. So may I achieve satisfaction for myself and gratitude from those around me.

I ask this in Jesus' name, Amen.

(87) When disillusioned with life

I do not know what is wrong, Lord, but at this moment I feel disillusioned with life. Is it that I am just physically tired with overwork and lack of rest, Lord? Am I mentally wearied with trying to work with difficult people? I am certainly spiritually weary: I have no positive feelings towards living, no sense of meaning in relation to what I am doing, no inspiration lifting me out of the boredom of routine existence. I am at a low point, O God, and in my need, I cry out for your help.

I think of your servant, Elijah, Lord, who was so fed up at being left to fight the prophets of Baal on his own. "Lord, take away my life" he cries. I am intrigued by the first instructions he received from the angelic presence. Take some rest and have some food, the angel says. Surely Elijah would have been told to "take (his situation) to the Lord in prayer", but not so. He may have physical needs that require help first. I try to understand this and do what Elijah is told to do. Then, Lord, I am perhaps more ready for the spiritual part of the prophet's experience. Elijah learns that he should not look to the drama of hurricane, earthquake or fire for the presence of God. He should simply listen to the still, small voice within.

Perhaps I too expect your miracles to be in cataclysmic events whose very trauma will compel me to believe. Perhaps I too need to be quiet, listen and receive. Be still, and know that you are God, indeed!

Thanks be to you, O God, who gives us the victory.

In Jesus' name, Amen.

(88) When facing temptation

When I read in your Word, O God, that Jesus was "tempted like as we are", my heart fills with gratitude. Our Lord was so truly human that he felt the full force of temptation. He can therefore understand our human experience. That he did no sin is, in this context, irrelevant. Because, O God, he was so tempted, we know that he understands what temptation means. This encourages us greatly, Lord. Not only are you "unfailing love", you have an understanding heart.

The sheer power of temptation frightens me, O Lord, as does its constant presence with me. The passing of the years, sadly, makes its power no less. The detail may change; temptation itself is never absent. Human being that I am, the original sin of Adam corrupting me, the pressure to yield to temptation will never leave me.

Thus tainted, Lord, my desires in question, my motives dubious, my imagination suspect, my need for your help is ever present. I cannot avoid being tempted, Lord. Let the grace that is sufficient be ever with me so that, in temptation's hour, I avoid sin.

Let me never feel helpless or hopeless when temptation comes. Fortify me with your saving grace. May I "pray without ceasing", be diligent in worship, and always stay close to your Word.

Where temptation and sin abound, may grace so much more abound. So may temptation be, not a time of defeat, but one of victory.

Through Jesus Christ, my Lord, Amen.

(89) With a guilty conscience

"Have mercy on me, O God, according to your unfailing love". So prayed your servant, David, when his sin with Bathsheba, Uriah's wife, lay heavily on his heart and mind. The burden of guilt in my conscience, Lord, leads me too to seek your forgiveness. I am so aware of my failures and shortcomings. Nor is it only particular sins that trouble me, Lord. I am all too conscious that I am part of "corrupted" humanity. For the creation story presents the truth of which we must all be conscious, that "all have sinned and come short of the glory of God". I know this and confess it.

It is then with some degree of empathy that I repeat David's prayer. "Create in me a clean heart, O God, and renew a right spirit within me. Do not cast me from your presence and take not your Holy Spirit from me".

For the coming of the Holy Spirit I give you thanks, O God. Let that Spirit come as a fire, purging me from all uncleanness; renewing me with Pentecostal power; bringing about that new creation made possible "in Christ", restoring my inner peace. Then shall I know that my relationship with you, Lord, is intact and I am whole again.

Let this be your benediction, Lord: "May the peace of God that is beyond understanding, keep my heart and mind in the knowledge and love of God and of our Lord, Jesus Christ". Amen, so let it be.

(90) On a retreat

Here in a place, long set apart for a time of retreat, Lord, I give myself, for these seven days, to reflection, meditation, prayer and quietness. I do this of choice, Lord, for I know my need. A spiritual dryness has overtaken me, Lord. I have been too much involved in the business of the world, a world in which, however hard I fight against it, one's heart is hardened and one's mind is corrupted. The struggle to survive in a ruthless world breeds selfishness and self-centredness. I give you thanks that I recognise what is happening to me, what my urgent need is and how desperately I need to go to "a desert place". So here I am, Lord. "I need you, oh, I need you", as the old hymn says.

I thank you, Lord, for this holy place, where down the ages monks and nuns have prayed and worshipped. It is a place where prayer has been wont to be made, a place of sacramental worship, a theatre of natural drama, truly a house of God. So, here alone, or in the silent company of others in spiritual need, I can feast on pure air, breathe the wind of the Spirit and so make all things new. What a privilege it is to be here! What joy! What bliss!

"Rejoice evermore! Pray unceasingly! In everything, give thanks!" So your servant, Paul, wrote to his friends in Thessalonica. May I, today, here in this quiet place, do as he says.

Through Jesus Christ, my Lord, Amen.

(91) When prayer is not answered

O God, I am in despair. I believe you are a God who hears our prayers. Believing sincerely in this, I have brought the needs of a loved one to the throne of grace… many times. That loved one is ill, Lord, desperately ill. I have pleaded with you for that loved one, but no answer comes. Where are you, Lord?

To take Jesus at his word is of the essence of my faith, O God, and that word is crystal clear. Whatever I ask for in his name, you will do it, Jesus says. "Whatever you ask for in Jesus' name, believing you shall receive, you shall receive", he says again. In my heart of hearts, I believe this, Lord. Yet my loved one is not getting better.

Where am I failing, Lord? Is my praying insincere? Am I asking in the wrong spirit? Am I asking for something I should not seek? Yet I am asking in Jesus' name, but no answer comes, hence my despair, Lord.

I cry out for your help, Lord. Dimly, I sense that that help will come from "turning my eyes upon Jesus", as the old chorus says. And in that faith, I see him in the Garden of Gethsemane, the sweat pouring off him "like drops of blood" as he struggles to know your will and to obey it. I see him on the cross, crying out: "My God, my God, why have you forsaken me?" Then I return to Gethsemane to hear him say: "Not my will but yours, be done". I, too, must make that leap of faith.

I do not understand, Lord, but I do, in faith, believe.

Your will, O God, be done.

Through Jesus Christ, our Lord, Amen.

(92) When prayer is answered

"To God be the glory, great things he has done". I sing this out spontaneously, O God, because you have answered my prayer. I was in deep distress, Lord, over a family situation. I could not see a solution to the problem which had arisen, but taking it all to the Lord in prayer, I now find the longed for answer has come. With all my heart, I say: "Thanks be to God".

I live my life, Lord, on the foundation of belief in prayer. I always read what Jesus said about faith in you with eager anticipation. I am always ready to take him at his word. When he talks of faith equal to "a grain of mustard seed" working miracles, I believe him, O God. And I am grateful to have seen miracles take place after such a prayer, positive changes, astonishing miracles of healing, wonderful moments of blessing. At all such times, I want to cry out: "Hallelujah! Lord!"

It is true, O Lord, that we "only see through a glass, darkly", that we are only permitted to see "in part" and not, as you see it, the whole. There are therefore times when the answer for which we yearn does not come. Give us, God, the faith to cope with these limitations and to be able to continue in faith until you bring about "the fullness of the time", the right time according to your will. Then may we replace our puzzlement with understanding and our disappointment with peace. Our prayers, Lord, must always be offered in terms of the condition: "if it be your will", Lord, believing your will is for our good.

Create for us, O Lord, a relationship with you in which we have total trust. May my faith be a response to your grace. And when my prayers are answered, may I be filled with gratitude. As I am, this day, Lord.

Through Jesus Christ, my Lord, Amen.

(93) Before reading the Bible

It is the evening hour, O God, and time to read a daily portion of your Word before laying my prayers at the throne of grace. I thank you, Lord, for the wonder of the Bible, its beauty and grandeur, the devotional magic of the Psalms, the zeal and fire of the prophets, the profound simplicity of the Gospels. How I love too the story of the early church and the wisdom and insight of your servant, Paul. For what I read tonight, Lord, I give you thanks.

This book is your inspired word, O God, but its inspiration does not lie in the letters on the page. That comes only when what is written there is read under the guidance of your Holy Spirit. Then is the page illumined! Then I will understand and be blessed! Give me then an expectant mind, a willingness to learn, and an adoring heart, so that seeing, I shall indeed see and hearing, I shall most certainly hear. Make this your Word a means of grace for me, a vehicle of truth, a stimulus to action. So may this time of meditation on your word deepen my commitment to you, Lord.

I thank you, Lord, for scholars and teachers who can open up for me, the treasures of the Word, who can show me the developing understanding of your will in the story of your "chosen people", who can interpret for me the signs and wonders demonstrated by the One, whom simple men came to see as their Saviour and their Lord.

For "the Word became flesh and dwelt among us, full of grace and truth and we beheld his glory".

This prayer I ask in Jesus' name, Amen.

(94) Before going to church

"Worship the Lord in the beauty of holiness". Lord, may it be in this spirit I prepare to go to church today. There is so much I must set aside and leave behind as I prepare myself for worship. There are all the practical, everyday things that, for this period of time, I must forget. There are all the worldly ways and habits that occupy so much of my attention, that I must leave behind. This is a time, not for the things which are temporal, but for the things which are eternal. For now, I must truly "seek first the kingdom and its righteousness" and let the "other things" take second place.

O God, I thank you for the opportunity to worship you, to dwell on the wonder and beauty of holiness, to encounter again your unfailing love. What a privilege it is to keep deliberately looking to Jesus, the be-all and end-all of our faith! How moving are the spiritual songs we sing! How comforting is the sense of the Spirit! O God, make real my sense of belonging to God's people, the richness of the fellowship of the redeemed, the atmosphere of holy things. Here, touching and handling things unseen, my jaded spirit can rise to new heights. How good it is to enter your courts with praise and waiting there, to "mount up with wings as eagles, to run and not be weary, to walk and not feel faint"!

Let these not be the feelings of the moment, O Lord, but rather let there be the transformation of the whole of my life, so that, coming again into the world outside, I will be seen to be a "new creation". May I, through worship, become a greater blessing to others and a more serene person in myself.

Through Jesus Christ, my Lord, Amen.

(95) Before Holy Communion

"Come unto me, all you who are weary and burdened", Jesus said. I hope sincerely that, in your sacramental presence, I will be able to find new life. It is, therefore, with a truly grateful heart that I come to communion to remember Jesus and what he said, to reflect anew on what he did for us all. In sharing the bread and wine, the chosen symbols of his sacrificial death, I desperately want to rediscover my faith. For that opportunity, O God, I give you thanks and praise.

It is with sincerity I now say my prayer of confession. Made free in the words of absolution, I surrender myself to your grace and, in an act of trust, I say that I will, with your help, "labour for you and ask for no reward". So be it, Lord.

Meditating on the solemn act of remembrance and resolution in which I am taking part, I ponder the mystery with which I am confronted. "There was no other good enough to pay the price of sin", the old hymn says. This, I truly believe, is the very heart of the Gospel. Somehow, Lord, in what happened on Calvary and in the Garden of the Resurrection, there was done for us what we could never do for ourselves. Blessed are we if, though we do not wholly understand it, we believe it to be true.

So I, with all my heart, now share in this holy act, O God. Deliberately, as a duty and responsibility, I take time to intercede for others. And when your Word is proclaimed, as before communion it must be, I listen to it with a sense of continuing benediction.

I leave for home with a sense of having "touched and handled things unseen".

Through Jesus Christ, our Lord. Amen.

(96) After worship

"Where two or three are gathered together" in Jesus' name, he will be there, he has told us. As I leave the house of God this morning, I thank you, O God, for that promise. I believe in my heart that we have been "with Jesus". And those who have been in the company of our Lord, will reflect it in their lives.

It was "with one accord" that, from those early days in the life of the church, true servants of you, our God, gathered together to pray, to break bread, and to share their possessions. As it was in ages past, so is it now. Those who love the Lord will meet together in churches, in houses to worship you, O God, and to dedicate themselves to commitment and discipleship. In such gatherings is true fellowship demonstrated, the meaning of communion made incarnate.

To meet together, sing together, pray together, and commune together, is to create the fertile ground in which mission and service can take root, Lord, one called to preach, one called to evangelise, one called to teach. From the healing community which your church ought to be, will come the ministry of reconciliation, the call to social action and the creation of charitable giving. In that community, gifts of many kinds will be discovered and dedicated to your cause. Such is the power and potential of a worshipping community, filled by the Holy Spirit.

For the privilege of worshipping today, Lord, I give you heartfelt praise. May I leave your house the more determined "to serve you as you deserve", more overflowing with true Christian love than I ever was before.

I ask this prayer in Jesus' name, Amen.

(97) On renewing commitment

It is my joy, O God, that I came to understand and accept the Christian faith a long time ago. It is my responsibility to renew my commitment regularly so that I keep "pressing toward the mark for the prize of the high calling of God in Christ Jesus". I keep those words very much in mind as it is so easy, Lord, for conviction to cool and standards to slip. I therefore pray for the wind of the Spirit to help me re-fix my eyes upon Jesus, "the author and finisher of our faith".

How subtle is temptation, Lord! Did the Lord Jesus not find it so when "Satan led him into the wilderness" there to attack him so sharply and so subtly, appealing to his self-interest, encouraging him to abuse his God-given powers, offering him the rewards of earthly power? If even your Son, Jesus, could be attacked by the tempter, how much more will a mere human being like myself be vulnerable to worldly attractions, to seductive sins? How willingly I confess that I am too weak in the face of temptation. And even when I aspire to the highest ideals, how easy it is for me to be corrupted, Lord.

I give you thanks for the way the Lord Jesus resorted to your Word in defeating the tempter. Help me, too, to call earnestly on all the means of grace, given to us in our continual contest with sin. I thank you for the power of your holy Word, a veritable "sword of the Spirit". I thank you for the refuge of prayer, providing me with the catharsis of confession and the affirmation of absolution. And I thank you for the sacrament of communion through which I can draw strength and determination.

So may the commitment to you which I renew today represent the sincerity of my faith and the desire to serve you more fully.

I ask it in Jesus' name, Amen.

(98) When in group meditation

Blessed indeed is the time appointed for our Meditation. To be with like-minded people committed to contemplation together is for me, Lord, one of the sacred times in life. For a long time now we have met together, every month, to give one hour to corporate meditation. For that hour we shall usually be silent, a profound and meaningful silence in which our souls are restored. It is a time when we stop thinking simply to be with you, our God, in silent and adoring contemplation.

How important it is for me, Lord, to engage in such devotion. In a busy life it is so easy to be like Martha, "careful and troubled about many things". It is not that all the endless things we have to do, do not matter. They do. But they must not so occupy us that we fail to look after the "better things". Our meditation is about those better things, the things which Mary cherished, the things which Jesus said would not be taken from her. Let them never, Lord, be taken from us.

I feel the need of this time of contemplation all the more, Lord, because our world can be such a tawdry place. The emphasis on sex and violence in the media, the endless "fightings" as James described them, bringing death to many and wounds to more, the sheer insensitivity of so many in society today; all this combines to bring about a world devoid of humanity, modesty, humility and grace so that, all the more, we need to have access to holiness. And this we can find only when we come, in meditation and contemplation, into your nearer presence.

So, Lord, I value, beyond measure, our time of silent reflection together and I come away from it, sanctified and blessed. The "other things" must occupy my attention again, but they will be confined to their rightful place. The things that are eternal have the ultimate priority.

In Jesus' name, Amen.

(99) In the eventide

"Abide with me, fast falls the eventide": this is my prayer to you, O God. How important is that petition to people like me, now in the evening of their lives. Surely goodness and mercy have followed me all the days of my life. There have been times of ecstasy and times of agony, times of spiritual gain and times of spiritual dearth, times of achievement and times of failure, times of rejoicing and times of bereavement, times when all was well with the world and times of despondency and desolation. But, as I reflect back on the years given to me, I want to say with the Psalmist, Lord: "I will sing to the Lord, for he has been good to me".

The eventide of life is a time for reflection, Lord, a time to recall and dwell on the eternal verities of my faith. And so, in the eventide, it is on those "eternal verities", I take my stand, Lord, and I try to live by the teaching of Jesus. I believe with all my heart he heals today; I see his death, descent into hell and resurrection as his gifts for our salvation, for forgiveness, full and free. I believe in his risen presence and the power of the Holy Spirit, sent to be our Comforter, our enabler, our sanctifier. Honour my faith, I pray you, O God.

May your peace, O God, a peace which is beyond my understanding, keep my heart and mind in the knowledge and love of the Lord Jesus, and may grace, mercy and peace from you the Father, from the Son and from the Holy Spirit be with me in this eventide and forever.

In Jesus' name, Amen.

(100) A Benediction

"May the peace of God, which passes understanding, keep your hearts and minds in the knowledge and love of God and of his Son, Jesus Christ. And may the blessing of God, Father, Son and Holy Spirit be with you, now and always, Amen."

May peace be with you, wherever you are on the journey of life. And may those who travel with you enjoy the blessing of peace too.

"In everything give thanks" when all is well and life moves forward steadily and safely. "Pray without ceasing" when dark and dismal days bring anxiety, suffering, pain, bereavement and the dark night of doubt and despair. Wait on the Lord, whose grasp of you never loosens. "Be of good courage" for he will "strengthen your heart". May the blessing of the God of unfailing love be yours. "Let not your heart be troubled, neither let it be afraid". "Rest in the Lord, wait patiently for him". And the God of peace will be with you.

Wherever you are, "the Lord bless you and keep you. The Lord make his face to shine upon you and be gracious to you. The Lord lift up his countenance upon you and give you peace".

"May grace, mercy and peace from Father, Son and Holy Spirit be with you", …where YOU are.

I ask for this benediction through Jesus Christ, my Lord, Amen.